R.E.A.D.I. TO LEAD

A Pathway to a Successful First Year as Nurse Manager

By Lisa Gossett, MSN, RN, CENP

D1260635

ISBN 978-0-578-25055-7

GOSSETT CONSULTING & INSIGHTS, LLC
Marysville, Ohio
GossettInsights.com

Dedication

There are many this book belongs to. There are many I wish to show my gratitude, not just for getting this book to the finish line but for the commitment to me and my own growth as a leader. In your own way, each of you have helped me shine my light.

To my family – each and every one of you have lifted me up, tugged at me, and held me to my core values. You kept me grounded as I journeyed my path.

To those I've had the privilege to lead – Thank you for your belief in me and what we could achieve together. Thank you for the willingness to follow even when the path was unknown. The feedback you so willingly shared gave me insights that empowered me. You made me a better leader.

To my mentors, coaches and colleagues – Thank you for the unconditional support, for the advice, for the guidance and for the times you let me figure it out on my own. Thank you for taking a chance on me and investing in my growth. You taught me how great leaders behave.

Table of Contents

R.E.A.D.I. to Lead – A Pathway to a Successful First Year as Nurse Manager

*If you could be **RESOLUTE** in your purpose, **EMPOWERED** to do what is right, **AUTHENTIC** and self-aware, **DELIBERATE** in your actions, while staying **INQUISITIVE** to discover deeper meaning – what impact might you have on those around you or on patients coming to your organization for care? With these attributes, you will be "**READI**" to make a difference for the people you lead and the patients in your care.*

Introduction

Congratulations on your new position!

This is an exciting time in your professional career. The Nurse Manager role is a critical position, sandwiched between layers of leadership and those associates providing the product the organization delivers. That product, the delivery of care, is the reason the healthcare organization exists. Leadership, at the point of care, is critical. Great leadership is essential to great outcomes. There is a growing body of evidence that ties outcomes to the leadership style at the point of care. The evidence suggests that relational leadership styles, such as transformational leadership, have a positive impact on both the nurses' work environment and the patient's outcomes. In your role as Nurse Manager, you will have the opportunity to impact how patients experience the organization. You will be responsible for creating an environment where professional nursing practice can flourish and impact the key performance indicators that drive quality care – a very noble station indeed. Congratulations!

I have over 30 years of leadership experience in nursing. I was a Nurse Manager for ten years before making progressive career moves to grow in my leadership span and scope of responsibilities. Since my time as manager, I have only grown in my appreciation for the position and the significant impact it can have on the patient's care. I have seen the difference a leader can make when they are resolute in their purpose, empowered to do what is right, authentic and self-aware, deliberate in action, and inquisitive, always curios to discover more. In a national quantitative study conducted by Press Ganey and Associates, 80% of Nurse Managers reported limited orientation to the job and nearly half reported a lack of ongoing development. Professionally, I have leveraged resources to create programing to support managers in their work. Personally, I have invested time in coaching individual managers as they pursue their leadership goals. I have learned from multitudes of leadership resources, mentors and coaches along the way – trying, failing, learning and trying again. I have found success in my own career and in helping others practice the concepts and strategies that I share.

Edith Wharton, an American novelist, said, "There are two ways of spreading light: to be the candle or the mirror that reflects it." Through our leadership, we share our own light and inspire the light in others to grow. I love this metaphor, probably because it is directly connected to our professional founder, Florence Nightingale (one of my all-time heroes). There are two Latin words on top of the statue of Florence Nightingale in Derbyshire, England (her hometown) "FIAT LUX", meaning, "let there be light". She was known as the, "Lady with the lamp," giving hope to the soldiers in her care during the Crimean War. Still today we see her impact on our profession and on healthcare in general. She was no doubt resolute in her purpose, empowered to do what was right, authentic in her vision, deliberate in her care and inquisitive about the unknown. Through *Resolute, Empowered, Authentic, Deliberate,* and *Inquisitive* leadership, you will be *READI to Lead,* sharing your own light as you inspire the light and hope in others.

I am excited to share my own learning to help you be successful. In this book, I will share research, theories, tools and tactics. I will share the wisdom of many and integrate leadership concepts with practical applications to support you as you accept the responsibilities, challenges and incredible rewards of your new role. In the pages ahead, I will lay out a pathway for your first 30, 60 and 90 days, the first six months and first year in your new position. This is a time for you to lead yourself as you grow into leading your team and managing the business. The process, tools and tactics described here will help you build leadership that is *Resolute, Empowered, Authentic, Deliberate,* and *Inquisitive.*

To best make use of this book, I suggest reading it thoroughly, then going back through each section, using it as a reference to navigate your first twelve months. The information I've collected comes from a variety of sources and disciplines. I will share concepts that will be a great foundation for your ongoing leadership. Furthermore, the tools provided will be useful beyond your first year. They will help you build solid habits right from the start that will accelerate your effectiveness. Throughout the pages I ask you important questions. You will find these written in bold; they are asked to provoke thought and to help you reflect on your leadership. At the end of each chapter, I provide a brief 'to-do' list, I summarize any tools shared along with some quick hints. I will call out several books that I call "must-haves" for your personal library. They are particularly helpful as you build habits and further develop your leadership in the role as Nurse Manager. (I identify eleven, almost one for each month of your first year – you choose the twelfth.) My goal is to help you create a transition plan that will reduce your anxiety and increase your leadership capacity while you learn the necessary skills to lead and manage your team and the business. This plan will increase the likelihood of a positive impact; it lays out a clear and organized vision of your first three months, your first six months and your first year. It is a pathway for your transition success and *READI*ness to lead.

Embarking upon a new job is among the most stressful of life events. My first bit of advice is for you to acknowledge that this transition is significant. It is a critical time for you as a leader. Transitions can be even more challenging when there is a lack of deliberate intention to manage the first days, weeks and months in a new position. I have seen individuals with great leadership skill fall short when they fail to meaningfully invest in their transition. Once you start, it is easy to become flooded by the excitement of the new role or to get overwhelmed by the learning curve and the new level of responsibility. Creating a thoughtful transition plan before getting caught up in all of that can save you time and frustration later. You started your first, professional nursing position with a disciplined and deliberate orientation plan, you want to transition into this new role with a plan as deliberate. Your organization may or may not have an orientation strategy for new leaders. Chances are, regardless of the organization's new leader orientation plan, you will need to be responsible for leading and managing while you are 'orienting' to your new position. Your first leadership "to-do" will be to develop your own transition plan. Take advantage of learning experiences that happen during the normal course of your workday – they are critical to your development as a leader. You are empowered to take ownership of your onboarding. Give thought to the new role and how you will lead (and manage) yourself. This will help you meet the challenges you face more effectively. Take advantage of the insights, wisdom, tools and tactics shared to deliberately start your position with a plan to grow your leadership. My wish for you is to authentically share your own light to inspire the light in others. My wish for you is that you make an impact, that you make a difference, that you shine your light.

"The way into the hall of success always passes through the chamber of decision. Decide to be a success…" – Israelmore Ayivor, LifeSkills Entrepreneur

CHAPTER ONE
Leadership Foundation

Before I get into the nuts and bolts of your transition plan, I want to share two leadership models that I believe to be foundational to exceptional leadership. Among the wisdom of many leadership 'gurus' that I will highlight in the pages ahead, these two models represent the foundation of *READI* leadership. These philosophies shaped my approach and are threaded throughout each section. Servant leadership, first coined by Robert Greenleaf and *The Leadership Challenge*, based on the extensive research of Jim Kouzes and Barry Posner.

Servant Leadership

"...when you choose the paradigm of service, looking at life through that paradigm, it turns everything you do from a job into a gift." – Oprah Winfrey, talk show host, actress, philanthropist

Servant leadership has been around for a long time. Christians undoubtedly would argue that Jesus Christ was the ultimate servant leader. More recently, Robert Greenleaf is credited with coining the phrase in 1970 when he published an essay titled, *The Servant as Leader*, where he described that the best leaders are servants first. Greenleaf spent 38 years at AT&T, spending much of his time in organizational development before becoming an author, consultant and teacher. While at AT&T, he observed that the most successful branches were the ones where the leaders acted more as supportive coaches, serving the needs of the organization and of its employees.

Servant leadership suggests that leadership thrives through serving others, including employees, customers and the community. Greenleaf suggests that in our humanness, we exist in order to cooperate with others to achieve a purpose beyond ourselves. He asserts that our highest priority as leaders is to ensure the priorities of our teams are being served. His findings, at a time when the priority of leadership was solely achieving the organizational goals and the common leadership style was autocratic, were controversial, to say the least. The servant leader is the steward of resources and serves others while achieving business priorities. The servant leader realizes results through whole-hearted commitment to the mission and attention to the needs of their followers.

I first heard the term "servant leadership" in the early 2000s from Ken Blanchard. I connected with the philosophy immediately. Helping others grow, supporting others in their journey while together working toward the organizational priorities. Light bulbs went off for me. It made sense to the caregiver in me. As a leader, my role is to serve, and through that service, our collective goals will be met – individual goals and organizational goals. I saw connections to a couple of nurse theorists (yes, I do enjoy nursing theory – it helps me connect with the broader purpose of our profession). The first is Dorthea Orem's self-care theory. As nurses, we support our patients to be as self-reliant and as responsible for their own needs as possible – we support them as individuals. The second is Jean Watson's theory of human caring. According to Watson, caring promotes growth, regenerates life energies and promotes self-actualization personally and professionally. She also suggests that caring is mutually beneficial for both the giver and receiver of care. As a nurse leader, I have always considered my leadership practice to be caring for the teams that I am responsible for leading. Servant leadership speaks to the nurse that I am.

> *"If your actions create a legacy that inspires others to dream more, learn more, do more and become more, then, you are an excellent leader."*
> – Dolly Parton, actress & singer

In the book, *The Power of Servant Leadership,* published in 1998, Larry Spears takes Greenleaf's original essays and organizes his ideas into ten key characteristics of the servant leader:

1) Listening – the servant leader seeks to discover and clarify the will of the group or individual

2) Empathy – the servant leader strives to understand and empathize with others

3) Stewardship – the servant leader coordinates processes that responsibly use all resources

4) Foresight – the servant leader learns from the past, considers the reality of the present while anticipating future consequences of decisions

5) Persuasion – the servant leader seeks to build consensus versus using directives

6) Conceptualization – the servant leader pays attention to the work of the day while consistently considering what could be or where we could be in five years

7) Awareness – the servant leader has a deep understanding of the situation, feelings, strengths and weaknesses of themselves as well as those around them

8) Healing – the servant leader seeks to create "wholeness" for themselves, in their relationships with others and for the organization

9) Commitment to the growth and development of people – the servant leader commits to helping others reach their potential as well as themselves

10) Building community – the servant leader builds a team of people working together to accomplish goals

Servant Leadership does not imply that the leader should function at the whim of others, and it does not mean that the leader is submissive or weak. It means to look beyond one's own selfish goals and help others excel in their work. In a world where we need the intellectual horsepower of the entire staff to contribute to the success of our organizations, leading with a servant's heart will bring out the best in others, and ultimately help you achieve your goals. Practically speaking, servant leadership within the hierarchy of organizations should be looked at as a continuum, likely never fully realized. Yet, striving to exhibit the tenets of servant leadership supports a healthy work environment that elevates professionalism and supports quality patient care. Healthcare is the business of people working with people, caring for people. It cannot be about the business without being about the people. As a servant leader, you have an unselfish mindset: it is not about you – it is about the team and the patients. Servant leaders support the caregivers to increase their capacity to provide care.

The Leadership Challenge

"Leaders are made, they are not born. They are made by hard effort, which is the price which all of us must pay to achieve any goal that is worthwhile."
– Vince Lombardi, NFL coach & executive

Jim Kouzes and Barry Posner have spent decades researching leaders and leadership behaviors. Their research suggests that how a leader behaves explains the differences between why people work hard, how committed they are, and the level of pride that they take in their work. Leadership determines the outcomes that are achieved. One of my favorite bosses and mentors often said that all things come from leadership. She said, "Great things are rarely an accident and are accomplished because of great leadership, the opposite is also true." Leaders set the tone: they inspire others to struggle through changes they would rather not face. Followers follow because of shared aspirations and because they know they will be supported in the process. She may have been quoting Kouzes and Posner. The message she was relaying was, that I needed to determine how my leadership needed to change if I wanted to get different results."

Kouzes and Posner's *The Leadership Challenge* provides guidance, regardless of what leadership level we are talking about. It has given me direction for my own development for more than 20 years. First published in 1987, *The Leadership Challenge* is based on patterns discovered by the authors through extensive research; the 6th edition was published in 2017 with additional research that supports the original model. The authors found that regardless of culture, gender, age and other variables, the five practices in their model held true. These five practices are the behaviors of leaders when at their personal best. Kouzes and Posner also believe that because leadership is about behaviors, it is available to anyone who is willing to accept the challenge of leading. They fully support that exceptional leadership can be learned if the desire to learn it exists.

The Leadership Challenge identifies ten commitments divided into five practices exhibited by leaders at their personal best:

Leadership Practice	Leadership Commitment
Model the way	• Find your voice by clarifying your personal values. • Set the example by aligning actions with shared values.
Inspire a shared vision	• Envision the future by imagining exciting and ennobling activities. • Enlist others in a common vision by appealing to shared aspirations.
Challenge the process	• Search for opportunities by seeking innovative ways to change, grow and improve. • Experiment and take risks by constantly generating small wins and learning from mistakes.
Enable others to act	• Foster collaboration by promoting cooperative goals and building trust. • Strengthen others by sharing power and discretion.
Encourage the heart	• Recognize contributions by showing appreciation for individual excellence. • Celebrate the values and victories by creating a spirit of community.

Model the Way – Simply stated, the leader sets the example: "practice what you preach" or "walk the talk". Great leaders are consistent with words and actions. Their behaviors match their value system and demonstrate their aspirations. You need to have awareness and clarity about your own values that define how you make decisions in your daily life. You must define and communicate the behavior standards you expect. It is common for organizations to have defined these expectations, often found in value statements or service standards. You must have awareness into your own guiding principles and behaviors to ensure consistency with the organizational standards. Be deliberate with how you spend your time, explain your actions, share your expectations and leverage teaching opportunities. Understand and pay attention to your words – they matter. Your team will be watching you. They will be listening to you. The consistency in words and actions will determine if they believe you.

"My role model didn't tell me, he showed me." - Unknown

Inspire a Shared Vision – Leaders create followers by painting a picture of an exciting future that followers want to help build. Leaders wholeheartedly believe in that future and believe that they can achieve it. As a Nurse Manager, this may mean executing on a vision that comes from another level within the organization. If this is the case, your responsibility is to execute and solicit commitment from your team. This, however, should not stop you from having your own vision for your team that fits within the scope of your responsibilities. This means taking organizational aspiration and defining it for your corner of the world – connecting the dots for your team. Regardless, you will be more effective if you inspire commitment versus command commitment. Help your team envision that future: what it will mean and what it will feel like. Then, help them be a part of achieving it.

"If you want to build a ship, don't drum up the men to gather wood, divide the work, and give orders. Instead, teach them to yearn for the vast and endless sea." – Antoine de Saint-Exupéry, French writer, pioneering aviator

Challenge the Process – Managing to the status quo is not leadership. Leadership is about going someplace new. Your organization needs you to lead your team to someplace new. This could mean improved quality outcomes, improved patient satisfaction, improved turnover or it could mean totally changing a patient population or opening a new department. Look for these opportunities, seize them. As a leader you are an agent for change, questioning, challenging and seeking new ideas. It may include listening to the great ideas of others and facilitating someone else's innovation. As a leader you need to take risks and experiment, take incremental steps and find small wins. Most importantly, you *will* make mistakes and you need to gracefully allow for mistakes (yours and those of others); learn from them. This will foster innovation and will help you build a culture of safety and psychological hardiness.

"Never be afraid to try something new. Remember amateurs built the ark; professionals built the Titanic." – Unknown

Enabling Others to Act – Great things do not happen by individuals alone. Great things happen as a result of team effort, and healthcare is a team sport. With that said, do not go it alone. Be a collaborative partner, solicit the help of others, foster shared ownership and build a spirit of collaboration and interdependence. As a leader, make it the expectation that the team solves issues through open dialogue, explores multiple points of view and works together to resolve challenges. Share authority as appropriate. Teach your team how to make decisions, give them the authority to make decisions and let your team know that you have their back when they do. Develop competence and confidence while you ensure accountability in your team. Empower them.

"A leader is best when people barely know he exists…when his work is done, his aim fulfilled, they will all say: We did it ourselves."
– Lao-Tzu, ancient philosopher

Encourage the Heart – Let people know how much you value them. Be specific in your praise and recognition. It should be authentic and connected to shared goals. Show appreciation for contributions, small or large. Create a culture that expects the best and where the best is achieved through teamwork and support. Create community among your team and encourage them to celebrate each other. Celebrate the values and victories. Look for places inside and outside of your team to share stories in meaningful ways. Recognition that comes from you is critical, and, never pass up a chance to give your boss reasons to recognize and celebrate your team.

"If you don't create a great, rewarding place for people to work, they won't do great work." – Ari Weinzweig, CEO & co-founder of Zingerman's Community of Businesses

According to Kouzes' and Posner's research, leaders who use these practices consistently have a positive influence on others within the organization. Individuals report feeling more satisfied, committed, excited, energized, influential and powerful because of their leader. Leaders who keep up with these practices are seen as more exceptional leaders. Kouzes and Posner suggest that exceptional leadership practices can be learned. I particularly love the thought that everyone has the capability to lead, if desired, with the courage to accept the challenge, liberating the leader within.

Key Take-Aways

Both servant leadership and *The Leadership Challenge* have consistent characteristics. The research of Kouzes and Posner supports the findings of Greenleaf. They paint a picture of leaders that are resolute, empowered, authentic, deliberate and inquisitive. Resolute in their pursuits and in their purpose. They are empowered to take ownership for their actions, their own learning, for driving desired outcomes and doing what is right. They are authentic, building credibility to galvanize followers around purpose. They are deliberate in their actions, focused on accomplishing goals, and they are inquisitive, constantly looking for what is yet to be discovered. This requires self-awareness and self-discipline. It requires bringing people together in community for a common mission. It requires a focus on the team: empowering them, soliciting their ideas, listening to their concerns and supporting them as a way of achieving organizational goals. Exceptional Leadership requires ongoing development, the development of self and the development of others. It requires learning and growing from successes and setbacks. It requires pursuing a better future, leveraging influence over dictate. Exceptional leadership requires the courage to truly lead. The two models blend the art and practice of leadership, highlighting that in order to accomplish personal or organizational goals, leaders must work through the heart, head and hands of others. These takeaways will be woven throughout the pages ahead. They will serve as guiding principles behind the *READI* leadership I encourage as you transition into the Nurse Manager role.

Self-Awareness and Self-Discipline

Leadership begins with a look in the mirror. To lead others, you must lead yourself first. Leading yourself requires both awareness and discipline. Awareness necessitates a deep understanding of the core principles that guide your daily decisions, what you care about, what you value, what inspires you, challenges you, what you do well and what creates obstacles for you. When you are self-aware, you take note of who you are and who you are not, what you have and what you do not have. Developing self-awareness requires soliciting and acknowledging feedback from those around you – learning if what you are intending to project is that which is seen by others, learning if your audience understands your purpose. Growing self-awareness enables you to build authenticity, it enables purposeful and wise actions, it empowers you, it supports your credibility. Credibility happens when the understanding of who you are is consistent with who others think you are based on their observation, the consistency in what they see in your behavior and what they hear you say. Credibility happens with deliberate discipline and commitment. Self-discipline is the ability to motivate yourself and stay on track while doing what is right, even when it is hard. Self-discipline enables you to stay in control of yourself, your emotions and your reactions. Leading yourself with self-discipline allows you to focus on your goals while being consistent with your values and principles.

Self-awareness and self-discipline require a deep, conscious competence of how we, as leaders, show up in the environment we are leading, fully conscious and responsible for our actions. The concept of conscious leadership is an evolution of servant leadership. It focuses on total awareness and full responsibility for one's own reality. A simple explanation of conscious (fully aware) leadership is described in a short video "Locating Yourself - A Key to Conscious Leadership." The video describes a construct in which, simply understanding our 'location' grows self-awareness and thus empowers us. Envision a horizontal line: below the line we are defensive, closed to learning, and focused on being right; above the line, we are open, committed to learning, and are curious. When we can live above the line, we engage from a place of trust. We are open to learning and curious about situations and others. We are enthusiastic and have more energy. Above the line creativity can blossom. When we are below the line, we are committed to being right and we are defensive. Knowing where we ourselves are builds awareness to the situation and our responses. A simple concept, asking yourself "Where am I?" enables a quick reflection to build self-awareness, leading to more effective leadership. This video is available through the Conscious Leadership Group. You can find it on their website or YouTube. This concept is described more fully in the book, *The 15 Commitments of Conscious Leadership: A New Paradigm for Sustainable Success* by Jim Dethmer, Diana Chapman and Kaley Klemp. The first must-have for your library. In this book, the authors describe fifteen unique behaviors that support self-awareness and self-discipline. It's a practical leadership guide designed to help leaders become more conscious, take personal responsibility, and lead others more effectively. With deep awareness, conscious leaders take full responsibility for their thoughts, feelings, purpose and actions. Through their actions, fully aware and self-disciplined leaders are transformational. Self-awareness and self-discipline will empower you and propel you towards accomplishing your goals.

"You get the best out of others when you get the best out of yourself." –
Harvey Firestone, founder of Firestone Tire and Rubber Co

Build Community

A community is more than just a group of people together by chance.
A community is a group of people who share a purpose and a sense of
belonging. Community creates interdependence and supports the
ongoing growth of individual members and the growth of the group as
a whole. Leaders that create this strong sense of community among their
team are more effective and ultimately create a team that governs
themselves to do what is right.

To build community, connect your team's work to the larger
organization. Share how their work ties into the mission, vision and
strategy of the organization. Connect your team's short-term
performance indicators to the broader organizational goals. When team
members understand how they are personally connected to the broader
company goals, they are more likely to maintain their motivation for the
work. They are more fulfilled and engaged. Build a community where all
are working together focused on a common goal in support of one
another. Build a coalition of community members that are resolute in a
common purpose.

"Alone, we can do so little; together, we can do so much." – Helen Keller,
author & disability rights advocate

Focus on Team

Your success is entirely related to the success of your team.
Support your team individually and collectively, while ensuring they
have the skill, ability and resources to do their work. Foster an

environment where your team is in it for the team, a collaborative and supportive environment where members help each other reach their individual goals as well as the goals of the team. Seek their opinions. Ask and listen to what they have to say. Consider any relevant feedback (note – most all feedback is relevant). Be inquisitive, ask questions and seek to understand. Set aside your own opinions and look for opportunities to give deference to their suggestions.

Empower your team, create a collaborative environment where open, honest and constructive dialogue flourishes, where team members can easily raise and discuss issues and where they feel responsible for solutions. Encourage diversity of thought and out-of-the box thinking. Help the team consider every perspective when tasked with moving the needle forward. The final decision should be the byproduct of a collective collaboration and active exchange of ideas. People ultimately want to be part of a team that creates greatness. Building an environment where high standards are expected and fostered will be motivational. It will build cohesiveness and ultimately will achieve great things.

"The secret to success is good leadership, and good leadership is all about making the lives of your team members better" – Tony Dungy, NFL head coach

Life-Long Learning

Life-long learning is critical to our nursing profession. Leadership requires nothing less. Through learning, we re-create ourselves. Through learning we become able to do something once unable to do. Great leaders recognize that the ability to constantly learn, innovate and improve is vital to their success. Commit to your own learning and development. Model your expectation that everyone is required to be a life-long learner by seeking wisdom yourself. Be transparent, and talk about your own discoveries. Be authentic and vulnerable in your own struggles as you learn.

Commit to the development of your people. As the leader, learn as much as you can about each of them. Learn about their interests, skills, abilities and aspirations. As you better understand who they are, you can deliberately match opportunities for them and direct their development more precisely. You will rely on this information as you assign projects or delegate tasks. As individuals grow, give them more responsibility. Support them as you hold them accountable to goals or project results. Teach them how to empower themselves. Stop yourself from micromanaging and focus instead on coaching and mentoring. Regular, meaningful and constructive feedback is critical to your team's development. As you develop your team, they will develop their own leadership and decision-making capacity.

"Only the curious will learn and only the resolute will overcome the obstacles to learning" – Eugene Wilson, NFL player

Influence

Your role comes with a level of authority. That authority requires others to act on your direction. However, putting the art of influence to work will enable your team to develop in more meaningful ways and will create even greater things. Merriam-Webster defines influence as "the power to change or affect someone or something; the power to cause changes without directly forcing them to happen." Influence elicits behaviors and actions through choice rather than force. Influence over dictate builds trust, stronger team commitment and is a true driving force toward excellence.

Another book on the must-have list is by author Stephen Covey, *The 7 Habits of Highly Effective People*. Covey states that the real beginning of influence comes as others sense you are being influenced by them, that you have listened sincerely to them and you are open to their ideas. Thus, influence starts with active listening and observation. Once they feel understood, then, share the "why" with respect to them, with a genuine desire for them to have something better. Influence creates a mindset change. As a leader, you are more likely to achieve sustainable change when people think themselves into a new way of behaving. The most influential people do not change other's behavior – they shift their mindsets. Authority often comes from a person's position in a company. Influence, however, is blind to role, level and title. Anyone can be a positive influence in an organization and these influencers are difference makers. To influence, you must have credibility. Credibility comes with resolute, authentic, deliberate, empowered and inquisitive leadership.

"The only way in which one human being can properly attempt to influence another is by encouraging him to think for himself, instead of endeavoring to instill ready-made opinions into his head." – Leslie Stephen, author, historian, mountaineer

Courage

Aristotle called "courage" the first virtue. He suggested it makes all other virtues possible. As a leader, you need courage – courage to take action, to try new things, to speak up, to use your voice, to provide tough feedback, to allow others to act and to put your faith and confidence in others. Leadership takes courage. Nelson Mandela is a great example of this courage, he refused to be ignored, even when his government put him in prison. He said, "I learned that courage was not the absence of fear, but the triumph over it. The brave man is not he who does not feel afraid, but he who conquers that fear." Florence Nightingale said, "How very little can be done under the spirit of fear." Your team needs your courageous leadership, they need you to overcome your fears. They need you to be resolute in purpose, to be empowered to do what is right. They need you to push through uncomfortable and difficult situations and help them to do the same. Your team needs you to make difficult decisions and not back down when things get too hard. Eleanor Roosevelt said, "You gain strength, courage, and confidence by every experience in which you really stop to look fear in the face." She suggested that we should all do one thing every day that scares us. The more you step forward, take action and face your fears, the more courage you will build and the greater the results you will enjoy.

"Achievers are resolute in their goals and driven by determination. Discouragement is temporary, obstacles are overcome, and doubt is defeated, yielding to personal victory. You need to overcome the tug of people against you as you reach for high goals. Accept the challenges, so that you may feel the exhilaration of victory." George S. Patton, U.S. Army general

As you read the pages ahead, you will embark upon creating your deliberate and intentional transition plan. Your transition pathway will incorporate these principles. I offer tools and tactics to help you put them into action. Your pathway will include steps to help grow your awareness and discipline, strategies that will grow your team as a community and tools that reflect your focus on supporting and empowering them. Your pathway will include learning and development as you leverage influence. This plan will give you confidence, supporting your courage to lead, to share your own light and inspire that light in others, to be *READI* to lead.

As I was preparing for writing this book, I found the following quote in one of my many journals scribbled full of notes, thoughts, and the wisdom of others. It comes from the authors of *The Leadership Challenge*. The wisdom in it is the key take-away –

"Love is the best-kept secret of the most successful leaders. Staying in love with leading, staying in love with the people who do the work, staying in love with what the organization produces, and staying in love with those who honor the organization by using its work. Leadership is an affair of the heart."

Why R.E.A.D.I.

Leadership is a balancing act. It requires moderating our natural tendencies while incorporating behaviors that are uncomfortable. Leadership is situational and leaders need to regulate their style and behavior to the circumstances. The Nurse Manager is responsible for creating a practice environment where the nursing team feels fulfilled and strives for excellence in care delivery. The Nurse Manager must build community and create a collaborative culture, integrating the needs of multiple disciplines, while also ensuring their own team's voices are heard. The Nurse Manager needs to use their influence and proactively manage processes to ensure compassionate, safe and quality care. They must leverage learning to inspire innovation and creativity while adhering to established standards. These individuals are responsible for executing strategic plans of the organization while creating an environment of accountability and ownership. The Nurse Manager role is truly a balancing act, full of paradox and potentially conflicting priorities. They juggle an overabundance of balls based on regulatory, professional, environmental and organizational initiatives. The role requires leadership that is resolute and determined. It requires leadership that is empowered to do what is right, is bold and courageous. It requires leadership that is authentic and genuine. Successful Nurse Managers are fully aware, while inspiring excellence in the art and science of care delivery. The role requires flexibility to the changing environment while creating stability and a sense of hope for the future. And finally, it requires the ability to be inquisitive, constantly seeking new knowledge to improve care, fostering the development of themselves and the teams they lead.

"The challenge of leadership is to be strong, but not rude; be kind, but not weak; be bold, but not a bully; be thoughtful, but not lazy; be humble, but not timid; be proud, but not arrogant; have humor, but without folly." – Jim Rohn, author, entrepreneur, & speaker

The Nurse Manager role is critical to the success of the organization. The outcomes achieved at the point of care, where the Nurse Manager is leading have a significant impact on the success of the business overall. The Nurse Manager leads where the customer experiences the product the organization delivers – care. They are interfacing with the community in a very unique way. Department outcomes are a direct reflection of the quality of care delivered. The health of the work environment for nurses, the largest group of healthcare professionals in the health system, determines the outcomes of the entire organization. Leadership creates the culture. Leadership style matters. In a 2013 article published in the *Journal of Nursing Management*, Carol Wong, Greta Cummings and Lisa Ducharme summarize a systematic review of literature that studied the relationship between nursing leadership practices and patient outcomes. The evidence pointed to the positive relationship between style and outcomes. Their findings implied that efforts by organizations to develop transformational and relational leadership practices serve to reinforce organizational strategies to improve patient outcomes.

Servant leadership and Kouzes/Posner's leadership model both point to the attributes of relational and transformational leadership. Kouzes and Posner's leadership model is a significant contributor to the caring leadership described in *Relationship Based Care: A Model for Transforming Practice*. This book is another for your must have library. The authors connect to the profession of nursing in a powerful way. Illustrating leadership at all levels in the organization. Mary Koloroutis, the author of the leadership chapter states that, "Leaders inspire others when they have clarity of purpose, confidence and ability to influence others with a laser focus on what matters most: caring and healing relationships at the point of care." She goes on to describe the transformational leadership cycle, where leaders who create a healing environment act with purpose, remove barriers and consistently make patients and their families the highest priority. Leaders must be *READI, resolute, empowered, authentic, deliberate* and *inquisitive.*

Resolute leadership is admirably purposeful, bold, steady, determined, unwavering, and courageous. Resolute leaders are highly determined and persistent. They have an inner strength that gives others courage. Their fighting spirit will push for what is right, uphold expectations and lean into difficult situations and complex problems. Resolute leaders are clear about the goals. They are tough minded and make objective decisions. They care about people while addressing entrenched, cultural challenges. Nurse Managers face conflicting priorities routinely. The relentless pursuit of compassionate, safe, quality care requires resolute determination. Nurse Managers are required to uphold the policies of the organization and execute the strategic plan of the organization. They need to act with courage to champion change and overcome resistance. Nurse Managers are faced with difficult decisions and must act with resolute integrity to do what is right.

"To get through the hardest journey, we need take only one step at a time, but we must keep on stepping." – Chinese Proverbs

Empowered leadership is invested and enabled. Empowered leaders accept their own authority and accountability to do what is right. Empowered leaders use their voice with confidence. They understand that with choice comes responsibility, and they own the consequences of their decisions. Empowered leaders have a strong sense of character, hold themselves accountable and follow through on promises. They accept new responsibilities, are confident in their own decisions and show respect for other's opinions. They are principled, fair and consistent. These individuals are inclusive; they see the value in the unique strengths of others. They facilitate the development of others and create environments where empowerment itself grows. Nurse Managers must own the authority given, own the results of their department and inspire that ownership in their teams. They must take responsibility for their own decisions and the decisions of their teams. The role requires credible leadership to ensure an engaged and committed workforce that is dedicated to excellence in care delivery.

"You may not control all the events that happen to you, but you can decide not to be reduced by them." – Maya Angelou, writer & civil rights activist

Authentic leadership is genuine, wholehearted and true to one's spirit. Authentic leaders have a willingness to be vulnerable. Authentic leaders are self-aware and transparent. They openly (and appropriately) display who they are and how they feel. They inspire trust by sharing truths about themselves and promoting openness. They provide honest heartfelt feedback and build trusting relationships with others. Authentic leaders have a presence that is endearing and influential. They live in the moment – wholeheartedly staying true to one's self and representing their true beliefs and convictions. They appreciate the uniqueness of others. These leaders focus on the destination without losing sight of where they came from. The most effective Nurse Managers inspire greatness in their teams and influence others to rethink their actions. Leading at the point of care requires focusing on the people and modeling the behaviors expected in care delivery. Nurse Managers who are authentic and genuine show empathy, compassion and care while pursuing goals. They act with radical responsibility and grow responsibility in others.

"Authentic leadership is the full expression of 'me' for the benefit of 'we'."
– Henna Inam, speaker, author, founder of Transformational Leadership Inc.

Deliberate leadership is methodical, intentional, and mindful. Deliberate leaders are disciplined and solve problem through careful analysis and planning. They provide a sense of stability. They are process-oriented and enable others to do their work. These individuals maintain composure, are diplomatic, reliable and responsible. Deliberate leaders are teachers, coaches and mentors. They role model the behavior desired and are true to their values. They easily build credibility, encourage others, are independent thinkers, and take initiative. They create ownership and accountability in others. Nurse Managers are faced with implementing significant change at the point of care. This change comes from a multitude of areas in the organization. Nurse Managers are expected to lead teams to consistently perform prescribed processes. Maintaining compassionate, safe, quality care in the midst of change requires deliberate and intentional steps. It requires methodical planning and review. Nurse Managers must anticipate issues and proactively plan to mitigate challenges.

"Rather than just reacting to the waves of things that come, ride them with deliberate intention." – Craig Groeschel, pastor & author

Inquisitive leaders have a sense of curiosity. They are humble enough to ask the right questions in search of deeper meaning. Inquisitive leaders maintain a learning mindset and are open to new perspectives and questions. They are reflective and responsive versus reactive and defensive. Leaders with a spirit of inquiry find the learning in failure. These individuals are more creative and open to the innovation of others. Inquisitive leaders are observant, and see things for what they are rather than what they are expected to be. They create possibilities, inspiring growth in others. Leaders with a spirit of inquiry explore the meaning behind their biases, enabling them to shift their thinking. They build meaningful and trusting relationships. In the changing healthcare industry, Nurse Managers must embrace technology and innovation. The pursuit of excellence requires learning at every opportunity. It requires a humble and curious spirit. The inclusive, collaborative environment necessary to delivery exceptional care requires the Nurse

Manager to explore their own biases and build healthy interdisciplinary relationships.

"In times of change, learners inherit the Earth, while the learned find themselves beautifully equipped to deal with a world that no longer exists."
– Eric Hoffer, philosopher, author, Presidential Medal of Freedom recipient

READI Leadership is:

Resolute – admirably purposeful, bold, steady, determined, unwavering, and courageous

Empowered – invested, enabled, accepting of own authority and accountable to do what is right

Authentic – genuine, wholehearted, true to one's own spirit, with a willingness to be vulnerable

Deliberate – methodical and intentional, purposefully wise and mindful

Inquisitive – curious and humble enough to ask the right questions in search of deeper meaning

READI Leadership is a balance of attributes that exhibit strength and vulnerability, determination and flexibility, risk-taking and methodical planning, humbleness and confidence, courage, genuineness, self-awareness, curiosity and agility. *READI* leadership fosters engagement with accountability, enables achievement through team ownership, and supports innovation and creativity while managing process. It strives for excellence with a relentless pursuit of compassionate, safe, quality care delivery. Nurse Managers who are

READI leaders will inspire others through their resolute determination while empowering others. They will foster the development of their teams as they discover solutions to the problems they face. They will create a culture of trust and collaboration through their authentic and genuine leadership. *READI* Nurse Managers make a difference.

You can make a difference.

*If you could be **R**ESOLUTE in your purpose, **E**MPOWERED to do what is right, **A**UTHENTIC and self-aware, **D**ELIBERATE in your actions, while staying **I**NQUISITIVE to discover deeper meaning – what impact might you have on those around you? What impact might you have on patients coming to your organization for care? With these attributes, you will be **READI** to lead for the delivery of exceptional care and extraordinary service.*

Leadership Foundation

Actions to take:

✓ Reflect on your own leadership philosophy

✓ Envision the leader you want to be

✓ Reflect on your own READI attributes

Must haves for your library:

✓ The 15 Commitments of Conscious Leadership: A New Paradigm for Sustainable Success by Jim Dethmer, Diana Chapman, and Kaley Klemp

✓ The 7 Habits of Highly Effective People by Stephen Covey, an oldy but goody – hence, the 30th edition published in 2020

✓ Relationship Based Care, edited by Mary Koloroutis – this book connects with the core of who we are as nurses and is a great resource on multiple levels from relationships to outcomes and how we use resources to professional practice

Quick hints for success:

✓ Go to https://conscious.is/, click on the resources page and take a look at the videos available. They provide some quick review of strategies to grow self-awareness, authenticity and credibility.

CHAPTER TWO
Overview of The Pathway

"You have brains in your head. You have feet in your shoes. You can steer yourself any direction you choose. You're on your own. And you know what you know. And you are the one who'll decide where to go."
– Theodor Seuss Geisel, Dr Suess

Again, congratulations on your new position! This is an incredibly exciting time in your career. You are embarking on a rewarding, yet challenging, new position. Starting a new job can also be stressful. By building a deliberate onboarding plan, you will lessen the stress you feel. It will provide a foundation for your success. It will enable you to make a great impression and grow your leadership capacity. Transitions are crucible moments for leaders and should be managed in a disciplined, intentional and thoughtful manner. Everyone's transition is unique. As you read through the pathway that is outlined in the pages to follow, you may find some steps more meaningful and more applicable to you then others. I encourage you, however, to consider it all before you dismiss it. Your unique gifts, the position demands, the organizational culture and the teams you lead should guide your unique pathway.

I do not want to scare you and, transitions can go badly. Transition failures happen when new leaders misunderstand the essential demands of the situation or lack the skill and flexibility to adapt. You want to match your leadership actions to the situation and create the right change in the right way. With the overarching goal of your transition plan being to build momentum for your ongoing leadership, I will discuss how you can do just that. I share steps to take that will build your credibility, that demonstrate vision, expertise and drive. I share tactics to help you avoid getting caught in vicious cycles that can stall your effectiveness. Michael Watkins, author of the book, *The First 90 Days, Proven Strategies for Getting Up to Speed Faster and Smarter* has researched transitions for over a decade. His primary thesis is about being deliberate and thoughtful when starting a new role. His book and wisdom have helped me successfully advance through several of my own executive level transitions. Many of the concepts are appropriate regardless of level. My goal here, is to provide more specific tactics and tools for your transition. I leverage his research as well as other experts along with my own experience to tailor the process for your transition into the Nurse Manager role.

Each segment of the pathway supports the development of your resolute, empowered, authentic, deliberate and inquisitive leadership. Each phase of the pathway builds on the previous, incorporating key concepts to further develop your leadership for the next leg of your journey. The journey starts with a focus on leading yourself, then learning and building relationships to take necessary action to lead your team and manage the business to achieve results. Your time should initially be fully invested in leading yourself . Building habits from the start to understand who you are, what you really want and how you interact with the world, will support your ability to effectively lead others. It will support your ability to influence systems and processes to manage the business you have been given responsibility to lead. The chart below illustrates how your investment of time changes throughout your transition year. Notice that even as you complete twelve months in the role you will continue to invest a significant amount of time leading yourself. Great leaders are role models of their expectations – they hold themselves accountable to higher standards than they do others. Leading yourself means approaching every day with a desire to be personally better than you were the day before. Great leaders fully understand their values, they have morals and integrity to fall back on when they face difficult situations Leading yourself means holding yourself accountable every step of the way even when its embarrassing, uncomfortable and hard. If you cannot do the hard stuff yourself, it is impossible to inspire that drive in others. You will lead yourself as you go about your daily activities, as you navigate conversations, as you build strong collaborative relationships, as you lead change and influence new processes. The pathway will support *READI* skill development as you learn to more effectively lead yourself as you lead your team and manage the business.

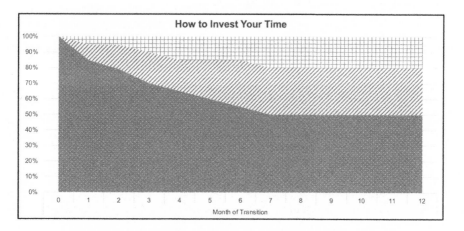

The pathway consists of the following segments:

- Before your start – **GROW AWARENESS & PREPARE:** The goal of this first segment is to prepare yourself for your new role. You will enhance your awareness of yourself, your leadership, your new role and the company. You will prepare yourself for the leadership transition and the learning curve you will experience.

- First 30 Days – **DISCOVER & DEFINE:** The goal during this part of the journey is to quickly discover what you can about the organization and your responsibilities in it: the processes, projects, people and culture. You will focus first on building strong relationships and learning as much as possible. You will begin learning aspects of the business that are part of the daily management required. When you understand your surrounding network, you can engage with those around you and define the priorities for your leadership.

- First 60 Days – **PLAN:** In this phase of your transition journey, you will become familiar with management systems and change leadership. You will gain clarity and agreement regarding what success looks like and what goals you will prioritize. You will build on your management skills and formulate the initial steps to achieve desired outcomes. You will continue growing awareness of the culture, processes, projects, performance and people.

- First 90 Days – **EXECUTE & ALIGN:** During this leg of your journey, you will begin to execute your plan and further develop strategies to meet your goals. You will clearly define and communicate your expectations. You will take steps to further build your credibility and align your team around your goals. As you continue to grow awareness of the culture, processes, projects, performance and people, you will design and deploy new processes to develop and empower your team, foster a collaborative environment and improve outcomes.

- First 6 Months – **REFLECT, ADJUST & EXECUTE:** This phase of the journey will focus on your introspection and vulnerability.

You will be guided to reflect on your results and leadership effectiveness. You will review feedback and make decisions about how and where to adjust your leadership in order to move forward more effectively to achieve your desired results.

- First 12 Months – **GROW YOUR LEADERSHIP CAPACITY:** The goal of this final stage of your year-long transition journey is to refine your leadership as you continue to reflect, adjust and execute. You will focus on further development of core competencies to grow your leadership as you lead yourself, lead your team and manage your business.

This process is intentional. The segments are building blocks to enhance your leadership and ability to manage the business, evaluating effectiveness and shifting as you go. It balances the tactical management tasks that you will be required to learn while growing your capacity to lead. Our professional nursing training guides us through a process where we assess the patient and their needs, analyze our findings and form our nursing diagnoses. We develop goals with other care team members AND the patient, then we implement a plan. We may shift that plan based on new findings or changed circumstances. We learn new skills and develop new abilities as new technology or care protocols are introduced. Our clinical practice relies on strong relationships with our patients and others on the care team. Growing and developing as a leader is similar. To lead your team and manage the business, you will need to continually assess, determine new actions, deploy those actions and evaluate effectiveness. You will be responsible for learning new skills that come with the evolving tasks of management.

The art and science of our clinical practice can be applied to our practice as leaders. Leadership requires an understanding of human nature, the spiritual-psycho-social element of the human condition, as well as the scientific method. Throughout my leadership career, people have asked me if I miss 'being a nurse' I let the sting of offense pass. (I will always be a nurse) and then I tell them, "I am still very much a nurse. I take the very best of what I love about nursing and I apply it to the teams I am working with." You got this too! Apply what you know professionally and use the deliberate process that guides our practice to guide you through this transition. Lead yourself through as disciplined a process as the nursing process. Be intentional and deliberate, resolute and authentic, curious and invested. You are empowered to lead.

"So never lose an opportunity of urging a practical beginning, however small, for it is wonderful how often in such matters the mustard-seed germinates and roots itself." – Florence Nightingale, founder professional nursing

Overview of the Pathway

Actions to take:

- ✓ Read through each phase of the pathway for your transition

- ✓ Take ownership and build your transition plan

- ✓ Get a notebook or journal – use it, write down your thoughts, questions impressions, and discoveries; this will support your development

Quick hint for success:

- ✓ Be deliberate about your transition – it is a big deal.

- ✓ Read through this whole book, you may pull things from future phases as you are navigating a current issue. Come back to each section and review.

CHAPTER THREE
Before You Start: Grow Awareness & Prepare

"Before everything else, getting ready is the secret to success." – Henry Ford, industrialist, founder Ford Motor Co

The goal of this first part of your transition is to lead yourself and build a plan. Before you start, build awareness. Get inquisitive. Spend time deepening your awareness, take notes – write down your insights. Gather a list of questions, jot down the additional questions that come to mind as you discover answers. Reflect on your purpose, clarify it so you can be resolute. Grow your awareness to become empowered and enable your authentic self. Be deliberate in every step of your preparation to accurately define your priorities. Stay inquisitive and curious about everything. Get *READI!*

Grow Your Awareness

I will discuss several aspects (a checklist) to consider and areas to investigate to be thorough leading yourself to become more aware as you assume your new role. I will guide you through a process to grow insight of your role, your organization and yourself. Lead yourself to learn as much as you can.

Grow Awareness of the Role

In their book, *The Secret*, Ken Blanchard and Mark Miller discuss "doing" and "being" – what you do and how you do it are both important. They suggest that the secret is to build trust by paying attention to both in every part of what you do and in every decision you make. The Nurse Manager role is a unique combination of management and leadership. The art is in striking the right balance.

That balance is dynamic and changes as organizational priorities shift, and outside forces impact the business and the team.

I like to think of the Nurse Manager role as a franchise owner. In this role, you will likely be responsible for a multi-million dollar business. Your organization needs you to take full "ownership" of that responsibility to support the business. Yes, health care is a business. Jobs and processes exist in order to support the business. That business is providing care to the community it serves. The business you will be leading comes with strings, like a franchise. You will not have full control over how the business is conducted. You are responsible for executing strategies, policies and processes that have been determined at other levels of the organization. A McDonalds' franchise owner does not determine the menu items and the milkshake recipe, but does establish the environment that supports the brand and the success of the restaurant. In general, as a Nurse Manager, 80% of your responsibility will be leading through execution of strategy determined outside of your scope of responsibility, and 20% leading your own strategies. In this role, much of what needs to be managed comes from organizational directives. Some, not all, of what needs to be led comes from outside your sphere of control. Your leadership navigating this dynamic is 100% yours to own. Striking the right balance regarding how you spend your time, how you interact with your team and your colleagues while meeting deadlines is yours to own. You own the culture you create in your department – in your franchise. The organization needs your empowered leadership.

You will face many challenges, difficult employees, financial barriers, unreasonable deadlines, or seemingly impracticable regulations. I am not sharing this to scare or intimidate you, but it is the reality of leadership. You have a choice as to how you will react to these challenges. As a leader, you have the power to meet and even resolve these challenges. Publilius Syrus, a Roman slave in the time of Caesar, who was freed and became a philosopher, illustrated this well. He said, "Anyone can hold the helm when the sea is calm." True leadership occurs in rough waters. The organization needs your leadership because of the challenges and the rough waters. They do not need your leadership to maintain the status quo, to canoe across a calm lake. Willingness to courageously face these challenges with compassion, collaboration, a focus on results and bringing your best self to lead – that is what the organization needs from you in your role as Nurse Manager. Be resolute in your pursuit. The role is critical to the success of the organization and is incredibly rewarding as you lead, serving those who are caring for the communities served.

"Leadership is not a job you take, it is a decision you make. It pays no money, yet has the greatest reward" – David Warawa, coach & business owner

You likely did some research before applying for the Nurse Manager job. Based on your findings, you made the determination that the role was right for you. And you accepted the position after it was offered. Now as you prepare to assume the position, as much as you can, from the outside looking in, grow your understanding of the role, beyond the job description and as an outsider. **What else can you learn about the position you are filling? What did you learn during the interview process? What more can you learn about the challenges and the leadership that will be required of you in the role?** *The Nurse Leader Handbook* by the Studer Group outlines numerous tactics that support exceptional care delivery. This is a great reference to better understand the breadth of skills required to be effective. It is filled with helpful tips and insight to help you lead your team and manage your business. A must-have for your library.

Another great resource is the American Organization of Nursing Leadership (AONL). AONL is a national voice of nursing leadership, with a membership of more than 10,000 nurse leaders from all over the country. Their mission is to shape healthcare through innovative and expert nursing leadership. This professional organization provides education and advocacy. It is a source of community and networking for nurses in formal leadership positions. In 2015, the organization developed a series of competencies for Nurse Managers, those with 24-hour accountability and responsibility for direct care. The competencies are organized in three domains: The Science, The Art, and The Leader Within. The competencies identify the knowledge, skills and abilities that guide the practice of nursing in the Nurse Manager role. The competencies reflect the leadership skills required, as well as the knowledge to support processes that need to be managed. Take a quick look at the AONL website and the resources available to nurse leaders. I have personally found this membership to be valuable. The resources offered are evidence-based and the organization is a great networking community for sharing and problem solving. The competencies outlined will provide a guide for your learning and ongoing development. And with experience in the role, will prepare you for certification in nursing leadership.

Grow Awareness of the Organization

Having an awareness of your environment – the department you will be leading, the organization, the profession and the industry will also help you lead more effectively. **What can you learn before you start? Broadly across the industry, what are the major challenges facing healthcare organizations? What issues is the profession facing? What global issues is the industry facing? What are the challenges in the community? What do you know and what can you grow to**

understand about the local workforce, pipeline and competition for talent? Before you start and with an unbiased view point, check out the Internet and research the organization. **What can you discover about the mission, vision, values and strategy?** Many organizations post an annual report – **what does it tell you about what they care about?** Many organizations periodically complete a community needs assessment and have it posted for the public to view. **What is the organization doing to meet the community's needs? What can you learn about the reputation of the organization?** Consider themes you are finding and make a note of what you want to clarify as you start. **How will your findings impact your leadership?**

Grow Awareness of Self

Billie Jean King said, "self-awareness is probably the most important thing towards being a champion." Regardless of the industry, greater self-awareness supports you becoming the best you possible. In the opening pages, I discussed servant leadership and *The Leadership Challenge*. Both stress the importance of self-awareness to leadership. Some might say it is the hallmark to great leadership. Why is this so important?

- Self-aware leaders have a better understanding of themselves. When you understand yourself better, you are empowered to make changes. When you know yourself, you know the unique skills and abilities you bring to the table. You can lean on these skills to navigate through your challenges and help others navigate through theirs.

- Self-aware leaders have insight into their biases. Understanding your biases can help you connect more effectively with others.

43

- Self-aware leaders have an understanding of how others see them. Self-awareness gives you the ability to recognize the impact you have on the people around you. Having objectivity and understanding of how others perceive you will help you read situations and interactions more accurately.

- Self-aware leaders own their weaknesses. With insight into your weaknesses, you are more likely to embrace others who have different strengths. You are more likely to accept other's ideas, ask questions and ultimately come to better solutions.

- Self-aware leaders understand their opportunities without shaming themselves. Understanding your humanness and giving yourself grace enables you to forgive others and learn from any situation. This self-awareness leads to self-accountability and that goes a long way when supporting positive and productive behaviors. Positive and productive relationships enable achievements.

- Self-aware leaders understand and interact more effectively with their constituents. Self-awareness gives you the capacity to empathize, adapt behavior, effectively communicate and grow your team.

At its core, self-awareness fosters credibility, trust and offers far more than just another tool for success. Self-awareness is the foundation to resolute, authentic and empowered leadership. It fuels your curiosity and the spirit of inquiry. The journey of self-awareness will help you discover and experience the impact you want to have. Mahatma Gandhi said, "Be the change you want to see."

Whether this is your first, formal leadership role or you are transitioning from another leadership position, take time to do some reflection. Be deliberate and review your leadership. Be inquisitive about who you are. You want to have an understanding of your tendencies, the core values that guide your decisions and how others perceive your leadership. Take an honest look at when you are most effective and when things do not go as hoped. Growing self-awareness is a process. It is fostered by a habit of routinely checking in with yourself, striving to understand how what you believe and what you think drives your behavior. Pretend you were watching yourself as others do. **What do you see? What do you believe to be true about you?**

My father gave me a book shortly after being promoted to Nurse Manager, called *Soar with Your Strengths* by Donald Clifton. It really changed the way I thought about being a leader. I went from being in charge of my shift to being in charge of the unit without much thought. Reflecting after reading this book was the first time that I consciously thought about self-awareness as a leader. I began leveraging my strengths to overcome my weaknesses. I engaged with others differently. I showed more appreciation for what others could do well. I was genuinely more grateful for what they contributed. I sought out others who could do what I could not. I stopped focusing so much of my energy on what I needed to fix about myself and worked to sharpen the tools that I had. Through my own reflection and self-awareness, I became less frustrated. The relationships with my team improved. I became a better leader. If you are interested in taking a personal assessment, *Strengths Finders* is a great resource written by Tom Rath. It is based on research conducted by Gallop and led by Donald Clifton.

Clifton is now known as the father of strength psychology. The book comes with a link to complete *CliftonStrengths*. Taking the assessment will provide you with insight into your strengths. This is just a part of the complex puzzle that makes up who you are.

Prepare

You want to prepare yourself as a leader and consider how you will adapt your leadership. Prepare yourself for the learning curve you are about to embark upon. Spending time thoughtfully preparing for both how you will lead and how you learn will accelerate your success. Through this preparation, you will build a plan before you start in order to build a strategic plan once you start.

Start with your leadership. Following the process, you have spent time in reflection and can now consider how your leadership may need to shift as you assume this new responsibility. **Is this the first time you are responsible for personnel and performance management? Are you shifting from being an individual contributor to being responsible to lead a group? Are you going to be responsible for leading individuals that were previously your peers? Will you be responsible for leading other leaders? Are you leading in an area that is not necessarily your clinical expertise?** As you start this new position as Nurse Manager, consider in what way you need to change how you lead to meet the unique circumstances of that which you are leading. I am not talking about drastic changes – after all, it is your demonstrated leadership that played a part in your being selected for the role, be thoughtful about how you will lead as you navigate greater responsibilities and more obligations.

In her *Harvard Business Review* article, "Becoming a Boss," Linda Hill describes the mindset shift required for leaders when they move from being individual contributors to managers. She states, "Even for the most gifted individuals, the process of becoming a leader is an arduous, albeit rewarding, journey of continuous learning and self-development." Based on her research, Hill submits, commonly, individuals perceive 'being the boss' as something different than what it actually is. She shares that these misconceptions can derail a new leader's success. You need to be the boss your team needs you to be, which means understanding the interdependencies of the matrix of stakeholders. Your authority and power will come from your credibility, not your title; Achieving outcomes will come from your team's commitment to the goal, not from your control. You are leading a team, not just a group of individuals and you are leading them to an improved new state. Becoming a boss is a significant transformation. This fact is true across any industry. If this is your first-time managing people your transition plan preparation should include intentional focus on the significance of that transformation. **What does being the boss mean to you?** Prepare yourself by being aware of the significance and be open to learning about what it really means to be in charge.

Peter Drucker, the modern-day father of business management (he's written 39 books on the subject), is credited with saying, "that which got you here, won't get you there." Marshal Goldsmith expanded on that concept and wrote a book titled, *What Got You Here Won't Get You There*. Goldsmith summarizes 21 habits (behaviors) that are known to hinder the success of leaders. He argues that while habits may not have stopped you from getting "here" (your current level of success), they will not necessarily get you "there" (to the heights of success that you ultimately aspire). Many leaders fail to expand their leadership as they climb the career ladder. Instead, they rely on the behaviors that made them successful. They fail to evolve their leadership practice when the circumstances change. I have seen many new Nurse Managers struggle and ultimately suffer from burnout because they fail to consider how their leadership needs to evolve. They lead their new, larger span of control leveraging the same tactics that they used to lead their patient assignment, their shift or project. Times of transition are stressful. Stress has a tendency to push us into habitual responses. Understanding your habits and your go-to behaviors will help you deliberately build new habits. The famous philosopher Ovid once said, "Nothing is stronger than habit." Our habits shape our behavior and who we are. Be intentional about the leader you want to be. Be specific about the habits that are helpful and those that may be harmful in your new role. **What habits do you need to break? What new habits to do you need to build?** *The Nurse Leader Handbook* is full of tactics that can provide direction on new habits to incorporate into your daily routines. Be deliberate about starting new habits that will make you successful. Take deliberate action to build the new habits that will help you be the leader the organization needs you to be.

"Success depends upon previous preparation, and without such preparation there is sure to be failure." – Confucius

This is *important*. I encourage you to be intentional about the mindset required as you approach your first day. Our founder, Florence Nightingale taught us to be prepared. Although the nursing process does not specifically call out a "prepare" step, we do prepare. We prepare through our ongoing education to ensure that we know the patient population. We prepare by using resources as we look up policies, procedures or medications. We prepare in the moment as we center ourselves by taking a deep breath before entering a patient's room so that we can be present with our patient. You want to be as intentional while preparing yourself for your new role. **How does your new role require you to lead, influence, delegate and direct differently than your previous role?** Whether you have been promoted within your current organization, are starting at a new company, or taking a lateral move – the players, culture and expectations will be different. **How do you need to show up differently?** Revisit this topic frequently as the nuances of what is needed will become more evident as you move forward. Routine reflection is essential to self-awareness.

Another key to a successful start is to prepare yourself psychologically for the learning curve you are about to experience. You want to learn as much as you can as quickly as you can. This means you have to accept the fact that you are a novice again. Being a novice is uncomfortable, especially if you are coming from a role where you were considered an expert. Be ready for that discomfort, but embrace it and leverage it to your advantage. You will soon be drinking from the proverbial firehouse. Do not take yourself too seriously and find joy in the journey. Leverage what you know about Dr. Patricia Benner's "novice to expert" theory. It takes development, skill acquisition and support to progress from novice to expert. Just as you had a deliberate orientation plan when you were a novice nurse, create a plan for your new role.

Think about times in your past when you had to learn a great deal of complex information quickly. **What did you do to be successful during that time? How do you take complex sets of data and distill that information down to create knowledge?** Develop a learning strategy to accelerate your learning as you start your new role. This may mean you spend time at the end of every day reviewing your journal, looking for themes, consider your hypotheses and additional questions for further exploration. Your strategy may include talking with someone regularly about what you are seeing and hearing. However you learn best, make a plan that includes strategies that work for you. Build in refuel time. You need to maintain your energy level and that means filling your own tank thoughtfully.

READI yourself, consider the following checklist as you build your plan:

✓ **What did you discover as you grew aware of the role and the organization?**

✓ **What did you discover from your self-reflection?**

✓ **How will relationships change in your new role?**

✓ **How will your new role require you to lead differently?**

✓ **What should you start doing?**

✓ **What should you stop doing?**

✓ **What should you continue to do?**

✓ **How do you learn best?**

✓ **How do you absorb and assimilate lots of information?**

✓ **What happens when you are stressed?**

✓ **How do you unwind or refill you cup?**

✓ **What is most important to you?**

I will be discussing more in the next section about expanding your discovery, so that you can further develop your leadership plan. Before your first day when you will be required to hit the ground running, prepare yourself and build your plan so you can be resolute, empowered, authentic deliberate and inquisitive so that you can be the best you, you can be.

"It's not the will to win that matters – everyone has that. It's the will to prepare to win that matters." – Paul "Bear" Bryant, college football coach

Before You Start: Grow Awareness & Prepare

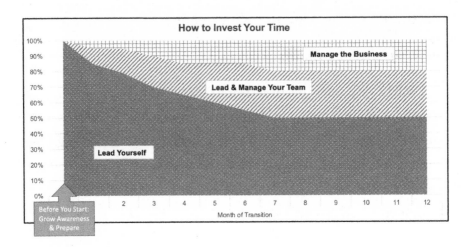

Action to take:

✓ Begin a journal. Take notes on what you discover, list your assumptions and questions

✓ Answer the bolded questions throughout this chapter

✓ Take an assessment (i.e., CliftonStrengths)

✓ Determine the steps you will take to transition into "being the boss"

✓ Determine the habits you need to change and the habits you need to start

✓ Create your learning plan

Tools Shared

✓ AONL Nurse Manager Competences

✓ Checklist to build your learning plan

Must have for your library:

✓ The Nurse Leader Handbook by the Studer Group is a practical guide to help you lead to improve quality, safety and service for your patients. The tactics shared have demonstrated results.

Quick hints for success:

✓ Build the habit of starting your day with a goal and ending it with a review of what happened – beginning these reflective practices will support your ongoing leadership

✓ Go to the AONL website: https://www.aonl.org/about/overview and click the 'Resources' tab. Click on the 'Nurse Leader Competencies' tab and download the "Nurse Manager Competencies" – use them as a guide for your ongoing, professional development

CHAPTER FOUR
30 Days: Discover & Define

"We were meant to explore this earth like children do, unhindered by fear, propelled by curiosity and a sense of discovery. Allow yourself to see the world through new eyes and know there are amazing adventures here for you." –
Laurel Bleadon Maffei, spiritual teacher

Your leadership brand and success start on day one. Be resolute in your principles, purpose and in your quest for information. You are empowered and you have been given authority – use it wisely to learn all that you can. Be your authentic self by genuinely sharing who you are with others – this will endear them to you and will begin to create trusting bonds you will need later. Stay deliberate in your actions and inquisitive in your unearthing. The goal of this part of your journey is to quickly learn all you can about your role and your responsibilities, and to build connections in order to grow strong, collaborative relationships. Your primary focus remains on leading yourself. You will begin to lead your team as you share with them who you are. You want to put that onboarding plan into practice, to discover as much as you can as quickly as you can in order to define your priorities as you lead yourself in order to lead your team and manage your business. As a leader, you will be expected to develop an action plan (or strategic plan) to move your area of responsibility forward. You probably have already generated some great ideas you want to see realized. **Where do you focus first? What needs to be addressed first? Where are the quick wins? What strategies are necessary to tackle those issues? Are there steps you can take that could address multiple issues in parallel? How best do you lead to influence the change that is necessary?** You may have some answers to these questions based on your interview, knowledge of the organization and experience. These thoughts, plus your hypothesis are important. If you have not already, write them down and hold on to them.

A common mistake for new leaders is quickly jumping into action. Although, I am sure taking some quick action is expected, I encourage you to be deliberate with all your actions. Pause briefly so you can gather necessary information and take the best steps forward. You will notice that I spend a good amount of time on the 'assessment' aspects of this process. With a complete picture of the people, processes, projects and performance, you will be able to move more quickly through the next steps of your transition plan. In the next pages, I share several lists so you can be deliberately thorough while gaining insights in order to define your priorities. As you execute your plan to quickly learn, you will find problems that need to be solved, opportunities for processes to improve and people that need to change. You will also discover people who are excelling. You will discover those things that are 'firing on all cylinders' and need to be supported. This analysis will lead you to diagnose the current state and then create the correct treatment plan by leveraging the strengths and resources you discover. The process will enable you to live your purpose and gain insight into what is yours to own. You will have the opportunity to share about yourself and your aspirations. The process is methodical and will feed your curiosity. It serves as the groundwork for your *READI* leadership.

Every situation that you will experience cannot be covered in a manual and every procedure you need to learn cannot be covered in one book. However, it is likely that others have worked through these issues previously. The first action I encourage you to take is to find a mentor, someone who is successfully leading in a role similar to yours. Identify someone who will act as a confidant that you can confidentially discuss issues when they arise. This individual can be your tour guide as you onboard, sharing some secret tips or tricks and answering questions as you embark on this journey. **Who is this person for you?** Confirm with your boss or ask whom they may suggest. Once you have an individual identified, introduce yourself, ask them to be your mentor and guide; schedule time with them as soon as you can.

Discover

"The real voyage of discovery consists not in seeking new landscapes, but in having new eyes." – Marcel Proust, 19th century French novelist

According to Merriam Webster, to discover means to "make known or to make visible." The process I outline organizes the discovery process – to make known the unknown and visible the invisible. It is important that you keep an inquisitive mindset as you take in all the information that will quickly come at you. Along with the learning plan you created, this process will help you intentionally examine the complex and multi-variant facets that shape the role of Nurse Manager. It will help you drink from that proverbial fire hose deliberately and without drowning.

If you have not already started a notebook or journal, *do it now*. Start identifying themes. Keep track of any questions that come to mind. Organize your discovery to leverage the learning. Just as the nursing process guides our practice through an organized assessment routine, this discovery process is as purposeful. I will take you through several key elements to organize your assessment data. I will guide you through a process using a checklist divided into four buckets: processes, projects, performance and people. This checklist is not intended to indicate the order of importance. It is not intended to be linear. You should plan to navigate through these elements simultaneously. Consider the big picture as well as the details. Think about things at the macro and micro level. You want to look for insights from various perspectives – across departments and levels within the organization. Take notes, keep track of your first impressions and the hypotheses you form. Be deliberate and stay inquisitive. Again, the goal of your assessment is to create the diagnoses to build your action plan and prioritize your leadership.

Organizational Culture

As a leader, you want to understand the culture of the organization, what it aspires to be and how it works to accomplish its aspirations. Understanding the culture is critical in your ability to lead within the culture. Organizational culture can be defined as the underlying beliefs, assumptions, values and ways of interacting that contribute to the unique environment of the organization. The famous quote by Peter Drucker, "culture eats strategy for breakfast" is powerful. Simply, it means that no matter how wonderful your plan is, its effectiveness will be deterred if the organization's culture or those of the department are not aligned. One of my favorite books on the subject is *Culture Eats Strategy for Lunch: The Secret of Extraordinary Results, Igniting the Passion Within* by Curt Coffman and Kathie Sorensen. The authors discuss how to use the force of culture to make any work environment a healthy place with inspired people and empowered growth. Culture is dependent on what is tolerated and accepted, not necessarily what is expected. In other words, a leader's "walk", will impact culture more than their "talk." Culture drives results.

Throughout each of the four "buckets" of your discovery, you will find things about the culture, within your department, that you want to change. You will also find things you want to keep and leverage. These are important discoveries to make. Stay curious. Through discussions, observations and readings, you will become more aware. Before you started, you began to inquire and gain awareness about the organization. Keep these insights and any questions in mind as you navigate through this discovery pathway. The following checklist will provide additional insights, about the culture and your place as a leader within it.

✓ **What is the mission, vision and values of the organization? How are they lived?**

✓ **How do your colleagues describe the culture?**

✓ **What should be preserved or changed?**

✓ **Is there agreement across departments and levels within the organization?**

✓ **How is strategy established?**

✓ **What are the 3 – 5-year goals?**

✓ **How is your department responsible for the goals? Specifically, how is your team connected to the mission and strategic initiatives of the organization?**

✓ **How is the organization structured and what is your reporting structure?**

✓ **Consider the matrix of relationships – the organizational structure is likely more than a simple organizational chart. How does this matrix impact your role and responsibilities?**

✓ **What is the organizational professional practice model?**

✓ What theoretical framework for nursing practice does the organization leverage?

✓ Is there a shared decision-making structure (shared governance) at the organizational level? Department level?

✓ What "teams/councils/committees" are you a member of? Should you be a member of?

✓ Are there "teams/councils/committees" you are responsible to lead?

✓ What meetings should be on your calendar?

✓ What "teams/councils/committees" do members of your staff belong to?

✓ What are the routines for team meetings?

✓ What resources are available for leaders?

✓ What software systems are used? Do you have the access you need? (practice navigating the software)

✓ What other questions come to mind about the organization?

Process

You will quickly want to get up to speed on how things work – in your department and across the organization. You are responsible for leading and managing the delivery of care. It is essential to have a broad grasp of the processes that support that care delivery. Understanding what processes you own, what processes you follow, what processes you need to manage and what processes you lead is critical. There are hundreds, probably thousands, of processes.

Detailed knowledge of all of them is not the goal. High-level understanding of how things work in your department, as part of the larger organizational eco-system, is the goal. You want to understand what is expected of you and your team. Below is a list that provides a place to start in identifying these processes. The list is divided into two parts, those processes that are associated with care delivery and those administrative processes that support the operations. It is not all-inclusive, as every organization has nuances, it does serve to generate further inquiry.

Care Delivery Processes – Spend time in observation even if you are being promoted within the department. Spend that time, on other shifts and in other roles. Stay inquisitive about what may be familiar. **As your team interacts with the patient and other departments in the care delivery processes, what do you notice?** Consider the following checklist to help you discover:

✓ **How does your team include the patient in care?**

✓ **What is the quality of the patient/staff interaction?**

✓ **What does the patient say about the care delivered?**

✓ **How does communication flow?**

✓ **How do others interact with your team and your team with them?**

✓ **How does the medical staff interact with your team and your team with them?**

✓ **How does interdisciplinary team coordination occur?**

✓ **How does the team work together?**

✓ How are problems solved?

✓ When something goes wrong, what happens?

✓ Are processes achieving the desired result?

✓ How does your team demonstrate the professional practice model?

✓ What does your team say about department operations?

✓ What processes create challenges for your team?

✓ What processes create challenges for other departments?

✓ How do interdepartmental conflicts get resolved?

✓ What are the informal processes that influence how work gets done?

✓ What are the daily management tasks that you need to complete?

✓ Schedule some time in two- or four-hour blocks during your first couple of weeks. Spend some time dedicated to observing, seeing and listening to how things work.

✓ Take note of your discoveries.

Administrative Processes – As a department manager, you will be responsible for ensuring completions of numerous processes (i.e. financial, human resources, purchasing), many within specific time intervals in order to maintain the smooth operation of the business. Talk with your boss and mentor about these expectations and the timing.

Talk with your peers about their experiences with managing these processes. Use the following checklist as a guide:

✓ **What are the approval processes?**

✓ **What level is approval required?**

✓ **What is the structure for team meetings?**

✓ **How are agendas built?**

✓ **How are team decisions made?**

✓ **Do teams work with consensus or some other means for decision-making?**

✓ **What software systems are used? What resources are available for you to learn the systems?**

✓ **How many staff (and what positions) do you need on each shift to provide care? What processes are utilized to determine your departments staffing plan?**

✓ **What are the personnel management processes you are expected to complete?**

    — Payroll

    — Performance management

    — Staffing & scheduling

    — Posting/interviewing/hiring

✓ **What processes are utilized to ensure safety/quality/service expectations are met?**

✓ **What quality management processes does the organization utilize?**

- Patient rounding

- Outcome monitoring/variance reporting

- Risk management

- Regulatory readiness

✓ **What specific financial management processes are you expected to follow?**

- Operational budget development

- Charge capture/revenue

- Financial summary review

- Productivity monitoring/variance reporting

- Capital budget requests

- Purchase orders

✓ **What are the informal processes that may influence how administrative work gets done?**

✓ **What other processes should you be considering?**

As previously stated, there are thousands of processes, and you do need to know the details for the ones you are specifically responsible for completing. Make a list of the processes you want to learn. Inquire about organizational resources that may be available to help you learn the systems and tools you need to use. Ask your boss to help you prioritize classes Create a time line to guide your learning. Schedule any classes you need to take and schedule time to complete any independent learning. As you establish routine management habits, manage your calendar – give yourself deadlines with ample time so that you can complete the work necessary before the deadline submission. Ask your mentor for help when you need it. They have likely learned some helpful "tricks" to expedite completion. Leverage the resources that are available to you.

Projects

As you assume your leadership position, you may be adopting existing projects. Members of your team may be engaged in projects. These projects may be departmentally or organizationally driven. You will want to inventory and get up to speed quickly so that appropriate projects can keep moving. Inquire about the status of these projects, use the checklist below:

✓ **What projects do you need to be aware of?**

✓ **Who is currently shepherding them?**

✓ **How are they progressing?**

✓ **Are these projects still a priority for the organization?**

✓ **Where do you need to intervene?**

The people leading these projects need to be on your target list that I will be discussing shortly. The people leading these projects will be helpful as you evaluate the status of each project.

Learn as much as you can so that you can wholeheartedly accept responsibility and manage them well. You will consider three potential scenarios: continue the project, pause the project to gain more information or stop the project entirely. Each of these decisions has consequences for you to evaluate. Consider thoughtfully. Talk with your boss about your thoughts.

Performance

Peter Drucker advised, "If you can't measure it, you can't improve it." Think about that – seems pretty simple right? Businesses measure performance, and as a leader, you want to have clarity about how performance is measured for you and your team. You will be responsible for leading your team to achieve the goals and you want clarity as to what success looks like and how it is measured. Consider the checklist below:

✓ **How does the organization measure performance?**

✓ **What are the key metrics you are responsible for achieving?**

✓ **How has the organization & your department performed?**

✓ **How does your team think they are preforming?**

✓ **How does your team describe gaps in performance?**

✓ **How does your boss think your team is performing?**

✓ **What is your boss's opinion regarding gaps in performance?**

✓ **What are the obstacles to performance?**

✓ **How are goals established?**

✓ **What happens when goals are not achieved?**

✓ **How do people, processes and structure play into the accomplishment of goals?**

✓ **In what areas might you find early wins?**

✓ **What processes are used to monitor and track results?**

✓ **How are results communicated & celebrated?**

✓ **What else plays into performance evaluation – what intangibles are used to measure success?**

As you begin to understand department and organizational performance against expectations, you will identify opportunities. You will determine if there is alignment with your employees, resources and processes to meet desired objectives. Creating channels to maintain regular feedback loops regarding performance not only facilitates transparency, it allows for the exchange of ideas to resolve gaps. What you discover regarding how performance is measured and how your organization and department are preforming, will be foundational to the goals and action plan you ultimately establish. Note your insights. Use the information to dig deeper and ask more questions. This information further empowers you to take more deliberate action.

People

Processes, projects and performance are key aspects of the culture you need to discover. These are things you need to master in your role as manager, and it will be easy to get focused on learning the tasks. You will feel accomplished by getting them checked off your list. Do not fall into that trap. Yes, you need to learn them. Don't focus on them to the detriment of the most critical component of your discovery – the people. People are the most valuable resource of any organization. The people are the reason your role exists. Your role as Nurse Manager is to enable the best work (the best care delivery) from your team. The measure of your success as Nurse Manager will be determined by how well your team accomplishes their work. I will go into great detail through this discussion of people. Why? Because The most important part of your discovery is getting to know the people. The most important part of your role as Nurse Manger is leading people. Be deliberate in the steps you take to build strong relationships. Keep the inquiring spirit as you get to know them. Be curious about who they are and what they want to share. Stay resolute in your pursuit to truly know them.

"The organization is, above all, social. It is people." – Peter Drucker, consultant, author, & father of modern-day management

Before I dive in, I want to stress the value of *Relationship-Based Care: A Model for Transforming Practice* again. I mention it here for obvious reasons. As a leader so much of what we do, how we do it and what we accomplish will rely on our relationships. As leaders in the healthcare industry, we are people working with other people, providing care to people. Our relationships with people are critically important.

The people are the ones you need to influence. Through your leadership, your goal is to inspire followers. Do not short-change this aspect of your transition. You have one chance to build a first impression. Focusing on relationships from the start will accelerate your leadership. Even if you have been promoted within the same department or organization, do not bypass this step – respect the fact that your relationships have changed. Be deliberate about growing strong relationships. I will take you through a discussion that will include identifying key relationships critical to your success. Then you will evaluate the current state and prioritize these key relationships to further their development. I will share a series of steps you can take to foster strong connections with each of them.

Identify Key Relationships – **Who are the people throughout the organization that you need to build relationships with in order to accomplish your work? Where will you go for honest feedback about your learning? Who are the key players you need to meet? Who are the influencers? Why?** Start a list of people to get to know or get to know better. This list will evolve. You will come back to it frequently, updating it as you learn more. The insights gained will undoubtedly evolve your plan.

Start that list. First, consider the organizational chart:

✓ **Who do you report to?**

✓ **Who reports to you?**

✓ **Who are your peers that make up your "first team"?** (I will discuss this concept more in a moment.)

✓ **Who are the medical staff members that you need to know?**

✓ Matrixed relationships – In many organizations, there is a *matrix* of relationships that you may need to consider. Matrixed relationships involve individuals who may have accountability to another individual but not a direct reporting/supervisory relationship. This may be true for you or members of your team. An example might be a respiratory therapist who reports to you as a department manager. This individual may also be accountable to a respiratory therapy leader as well. **What are the matrixed relationships within your organizational structure? Who are these individuals and who is their "matrixed" relationships with?**

Your success will depend on your ability to influence people outside your direct line of control. Decisions made by others will impact you and your team. In your process review you identified those processes that may be external to your department but significantly impact you or your department. Consider leaders in departments that are closely connected with care delivery processes and add them to your list. Identify those whose support is essential for you and your team's success.

✓ **Who are the leaders in those departments that your team works with closely? Who are the direct and indirect customers of your department?**

✓ **Who are the leaders in departments that are critical to your team's success?**

✓ **Who are the informal leaders that have significant influence in the organization?**

✓ **Who else does your boss recommend you meet?**

As a manager within the organization, there are areas that will significantly impact your work and how you spend your time. Evaluate those administrative processes discussed previously. **Are there departments in which a key contact person may be helpful as you navigate those processes?** Consider the following departments that you may want to have a key contact, someone you can rely on for information, questions and support:

- Human Resources – you will want a partner when it comes to addressing personnel issues, posting positions, interviewing, hiring and onboarding. Identify a key contact to help answer your questions and support your decisions.

- Quality, Safety, Service – you will want partners to help you understand quality and patient experience metrics, identify trends and issues, resolve concerns and improve outcomes. Identify the key individuals who support clinical leaders and seek to improve care delivery.

- Risk Management – you will want a partner to help address serious safety events or unusual occurrences. Identify a key contact for guidance when questions or issues arise.

- Compliance and regulatory readiness – you want a partner to ensure that your department maintains all regulatory requirements, to be in constant readiness for any potential regulatory reviews and to answer potential scope of practice questions. Identify the key individuals that support clinical leaders to ensure compliance.

- Finance – you will want to develop a deep understanding of your financial reports, how productivity is monitored and the connection to budgeting, staff planning and position control. Identify the key contacts for financial management.

- **What other areas should you consider based on your specific department and your specific patient population?**

Is your list getting long and overwhelming? Don't worry! It is best to start with a more inclusive list. You will be prioritizing it as you move forward. As you consider that prioritization, however, I want to share a paradigm that may disrupt the usual thinking when it comes to the typical hierarchy present in most organizational structures.

The typical organizational structure starts with the senior most individual at the top, with cascading levels of leadership and areas of responsibility below, connected by lines that demonstrate reporting relationships. In the spirit of servant leadership, I want you to consider that organizational structure upside down – with the most senior individual at the bottom of the page, supporting and serving the levels above. In the discussion of servant leadership early on, I shared how servant leaders achieve their best by serving others. If you think about your role as 'working for' those who report to you, your job is to empower them, grow them and ensure that they have what they need to succeed. You support them by removing barriers. They stand on your shoulders. For some fun, I challenge you to build your own organizational chart documents 'upside down'. Illustrate your own philosophy of how you see the role as in support of those you lead. See what kind of response you get from those who see it.

"Everybody can be great… because anyone can serve." – Martin
Luther King, minister & civil rights activist

Serving in relationships that are up, down and sideways – the servant leader has the humility, insight and courage to acknowledge that they can learn from people at all levels of an organization. They see their responsibility as a leader to empower, build the confidence, capacity and ownership of these individuals. Setting an inspiring vision, challenging outdated processes, helping others own the business supporting them as they take action and encouraging their hearts are just a few examples of an exceptional servant leader. Simon Sinek, in his book titled, *Leaders Eat*

Last: Why Some Teams Pull Together and Others Don't, describes the need to create a circle of safety. He tells us that this circle of safety focuses on creating an environment where we help each other rather than compete with one another. He suggests that when we know and trust the people within the circle of safety, we are more likely to freely exchange information and ideas that will move the organization forward. Now, consider how this paradigm from the typical organizational structure could change how you lead. Consider how it may impact the people and relationships on your list. **What names should you add to your list?**

There are many relationships that are important in this circle of safety. There are some I suggest you focus on growing first: the relationship with your boss, your first team, key medical staff members and your direct reports. I will discuss each of these in more detail. As you read ahead, consider what you know about these individuals already. **What more do you want to know?** Stay inquisitive and be deliberate as you devote time and energy to grow each of these relationships.

Your Boss – Obviously, this is a critical relationship that you want to deliberately invest in from the very beginning. This is a relationship you need to effectively manage. **In the spirit of that circle of safety and servant leadership, how do you serve your boss best?** In their *Harvard Business Review* article titled, "Managing Your Boss," John Gabarro and John Kotter suggest that at a minimum, you need to understand and appreciate your boss's goals and pressures. You will be expected to help your boss overcome their pressures and achieve their goals. You serve your boss best by accomplishing their desired results in a meaningful way. Your goal is to make your boss look good. Be an inspiration to your boss by how you lead and what you accomplish.

The better work you do, the better your boss will look. It's just that simple. If you and your team are firing on all cylinders, meeting the goals that were established and living the mission, vision and values of the organization, then you make your boss look good. Your boss will trust you to lead, you demonstrate commitment to the organization and you gain respect and influence. Additionally, your boss is able to share the success that you and your team created. Your team of direct reports is your boss's team too, and in the circle of safety, you are supporting one another to achieve the established goals.

"A perfect employee is the one who inspires their boss as much as their boss inspires them." – Unknown

Early in your onboarding (week 1), schedule regular updates with your boss – weekly if possible. If that is not possible, ask your boss how they want to be updated about your findings and actions. Validate how you will leverage your mentor for questions. You do not want to surprise your boss or get off track without some course correction if necessary. You want to understand how your boss likes to work. Ultimately you will want to negotiate your defined goals and action plan. Be thoughtful and plan for your conversations with your boss. Be your authentic self and ask for help when necessary. Do not fake knowledge. Allow your boss the opportunity to truly support you and your development as a leader. Build an agenda for these discussions that is intentional. Initially you will discuss your discoveries, your actions and you will clarify expectations. Once you get into a routine, include an update on results, project status, barriers and support you need.

You want to understand your boss's impression of your area(s) of responsibility and expected outcomes. In your ongoing conversations, you should have a clear understanding of resources that are available to you and your team. You want to know how your boss gives feedback. **How will you know if you are meeting expectations?** Ask for feedback regularly, even if it is given. Make sure your boss knows you are open to hearing constructive feedback and insights. Once it is given, be deliberate about putting the feedback into action. When appropriate, invite your boss to your department. This is a great way to share the positives, recognize team members and enable first hand visibility into challenges you may be facing.

Before I go on, I want to share more about a few fundamentals as you build your relationship with your boss. These may be basic and common sense, yet worth discussing as so many take for granted. As you transition into this new role, your boss relationship will be different than your boss-relationship as an individual contributor. In "Managing Your Boss," Gabarro and Kotter explain the fallacy of expecting your boss to be perfect. A failure to recognize your relationship with your boss as one of mutual dependence between two fallible human beings can be detrimental. You may fall into a trap where you avoid trying to manage the relationship or where you manage it ineffectively. It helps to think about this relationship as an interdependent partnership, where your boss maintains authority. Remember, your boss is human too. Like you, your boss has leadership strengths, weaknesses and opportunities. I have seen many leaders (including me) stumble with these basics. Below are some dos and don'ts to help you manage this critical relationship.

Let's start with what might hang you up – what not to do:

- Do not shy away – do not wait for your boss to reach out. Take the initiative to provide updates, and to be aware of the 'rope' you have been given and get clarity before using it.

- Do not surprise your boss – it is better coming from you than someone else. Be authentic.

- Do not discuss only problems – be solution-oriented, remember you are empowered.

- Do not just run down a checklist – focus on the important things, not just a run-down of what you are doing. Be deliberate in setting an agenda for when you meet with your boss.

- Do not expect your boss to change – you need to match your boss's style and meet those needs. Be versatile and deliberate.

Now, what to do:

- Do remember that your boss is human. Your boss wants to know that you see them as more than the person who does your performance evaluation. Be curious about them.

- Do clarify expectations early and often – this should begin immediately as you start your new position. Strive for open communication. You are educating your boss and others about your insights. Leverage your one-on-one conversations and team meetings. Be resolute and authentic.

- Do take 100% responsibility – own the business and your relationship with your boss. Own your responsibility to communicate and educate others as necessary. Lean into conversations you need to have. You are empowered. Take initiative and show your creativity.

- Do negotiate time lines and deliverables. Be deliberate.

- Do aim for early wins but remain resolute in your purpose and be empowered to do what is right.

- Do consider all stakeholders.

- Do be yourself. Be genuine and authentic.

- Do ask for help when you need it. Be appropriately vulnerable.

Be intentional. Grow your relationship with your boss. Build and practice these habits from the very beginning. This relationship is crucial to your success.

Your First Team – I want to discuss a concept that eludes many. Patrick Lencioni, author of *The Advantage: Why Organizational Health Trumps Everything Else in Business*, suggests that leaders must put the needs of the higher team ahead of the needs of their departments. This is the mindset of 'first team'. Your first team is the group of individuals who also report to your boss. These individuals must be included in that circle of safety. Although you may be a part of several teams, your first team is that of you and your peers that are driving change and meeting your boss's objectives – helping your boss be successful. You support one another when you are together or apart. Disagreements and conflicts are managed within the team. Your direct reports should see and feel that support that you give these other leaders. Your boss needs to see that support and collaboration. They want to see you aligned and marching in the same direction, working toward the same big goals. You will achieve commitment and loyalty, not just to the individuals and group as a whole, but to the organization and its mission. You will increase your credibility.

Within the typical nursing organizational structure, this first team may be expanded to the group of clinical managers at your level in the organization. It is critical that you see yourself and these colleagues as your first team – supporting, collaborating and working with them to address each other's concerns in order to meet the objectives of the organization your boss. Think about this as a team of individuals (you and your manager peers) leading and serving another team of individuals (those associates delivering care). Healthcare is a team sport, and you need each other to be successful. More importantly, the patient needs everyone working together to deliver the care they deserve. **How will you demonstrate the support of your first team?**

"No one can whistle a symphony. It takes a whole orchestra to play it." – Halford.E. Luccock, Methodist minister & Yale professor

A damaging culture trait that impacts patient care is siloed thinking, unresolved interdepartmental conflict and competition for favor. This leads to blocked collaboration across the manager team and departments. This is the result of managers putting their team ahead of their first team, and the higher organization. Unintentionally, this creates mistrust with other leaders and departments. It turns into a vicious cycle. Your direct reports are very important, but they are not your first team. It is easy, however, to think and behave as if they are your first team. You will spend a great deal of time with them, advocate for them, help them remove barriers and be in 'battle' with them. There will be conflicts between departments that need to be resolved. A positive relationship with you first team colleagues will enable a healthier resolution and that allows you to support your team even more effectively.

Mahatma Gandhi said, "I suppose leadership at one time meant muscles; but today it means getting along with people." I suggest that today, leadership is much more than just getting along with people. It is about trust and a true commitment to the success of others. Stephen Covey said, "Without trust, we don't truly collaborate; we merely coordinate or, at best, cooperate. It is trust that transforms a group of people into a team." Your responsibility as a team member and leader in the organization is to foster a trusting environment for collaboration to flourish. Patients and communities need and deserve their health care team to be collaborators. With a 'first team' mindset, your direct reports will see your trust in your peers, and how well you resolve conflicts with other departments. You will be modeling the way. They will see the expectation to work together and how to successfully cooperate across departments. They will see your empowered, authentic and deliberate leadership. You, your team, your colleagues and boss will be more successful. Your team of direct reports will grow in their leadership. Reflect. **How you have you behaved in the past?** Be mindful going into this position and consider how you will make others on your first team wildly successful. Do your part to create the team dynamic and environment you desire. Make these first team individuals a priority (use the agenda format discussed later in this section for your meetings with them).

"Personal relationships are the fertile soil from which all advancement, all success, all achievement in real life grows." – Ben Stein, writer, lawyer, actor, comedian, & commentator

Find out how your first team meets. **Does your boss have regular team meetings? How are the agendas built? How are decisions made and issues resolved? Are there organizational, manager meetings where all managers are gathered to discuss issues?** As you manage your calendar, make sure these meetings are added. In addition, you will want to start meeting one-on-one with members of your first team. Be deliberate about getting to know them. Be authentic and genuine.

Medical Staff Relationships – Another key relationship to consider is with the medical staff. They are crucial members of the care team who have significant influence by nature of their role and responsibilities. Other team members (including your team) will look to them for leadership. Who are the medical staff members you need to get to know? Developing a collaborative partnership with them will pay dividends down the road. Typically, it is the medical staff that has ultimate responsibility for the quality of care that is delivered in hospitals. They have been delegated this task by the governing board of the organization. The medical staff has their own leadership structure and those individuals who see patients admitted to your department are part of that structure. They want to be assured that quality care is being delivered. Showing ownership of their concerns, letting them know when you will follow-up and then following through will go a long way for growing these important relationships Your goals as you establish these relationships are to ensure they know:

- That you are the leader of the department

- That you and your staff will provide excellent care to their patients

- That you desire to make it as easy as possible for them to practice in your department

- That you will work with them to address any concerns

- That you want to understand the unique perspective they hold about your department and the care provided

Depending on the type of department you lead, there may be many physicians or just a few. Identify the key medical staff members that utilize your department frequently and add them to your key relationship list. Getting to know them is important. Be inquisitive – discover your department and the care provided through their eyes. Keep these individuals informed of related changes you plan to implement. When you have that trusting and collaborative relationship, these individuals can be your greatest champions. When they know and trust you, they will support you and your leadership. Include them as a key stakeholder for change. Leverage their influence and help them leverage yours.

Time is a valuable resource for everyone, including this group. By nature of the medical staff's workflows, you should not plan on a scheduled 45-minute to hour meeting with them. You will need to be creative and flexible about getting their feedback. Find out when they typically do rounds to see patients and introduce yourself. Tell them you would like to hear their perspective. Ask if they have time for a conversation and how best to accomplish it. I have used several strategies, from calling their office and scheduling time, to posing a question to them letting them think about it, and following up for their answer another time. It is important that they know you are the leader, that you value their input and that you are interested in theirs and their patients' experience.

Your Direct Reports – Another obvious priority relationship is your team of direct reports. This is your team and they are each other's first team. The more your team can learn about you, the more they will be willing (or not) to follow you. They are sizing you up and "testing" their willingness to follow you. **How are you showing up with them? What do they see? What do you want them to see?** The more you learn about the individuals on your team, the better you can support them. The more you learn about your team the more you can grow their effectiveness. **How do you see them interacting? How do they support one another? Do they share information about themselves?** Ask and listen. Your team of direct caregivers will see and experience elements of the organization that you may not. You want this to become known and visible to you. The more you interact with team members and encourage open communication, the more you will learn. Your visibility is important to identify issues before they escalate. Your visibility will support alignment and with your authentic empowered leadership will foster trust and autonomy.

As Nurse Manager, you have a responsibility for care delivery 24 hours a day, seven days a week. You are the link between organizational strategy and the point of care. Managing your visibility without being physically present around the clock, and falling prey to burnout is essential. Be deliberate – create a meaningful leadership visibility plan. This will enable you to share your authentic self with your team, will foster a trusting environment and will enable you to keep your pulse on department operations. This is critical to your success. Theodore Roosevelt said, "Nobody cares how much you know, until they know how much you care." Your visibility plan will help you show your team how much you care. You want your team to feel you care for them as individuals, you care about their wellbeing and you are genuinely committed to them. You want to create a safe space to discuss what is really happening and what needs to be addressed to make your team's work lives better and more fulfilling. You want them to feel your presence even when you are not around.

Creating a plan for visibility has several purposes:

- It enables your team to see and get to know you

- It enables you to see and get to know your team

- It enables you to see first-hand how your department functions and how your team interacts

- It enables your team to take action

Your visibility plan provides a disciplined and deliberate routine for staff interactions. It includes routine 'walking around' for observation and conversation. It includes talking with patients. It includes uninterrupted time dedicated to your direct reports in group and individual meetings. It ensures that you are talking with everyone routinely. It requires a process for capturing observations and hearing concerns. A good visibility plan also includes a feedback loop for any follow-up. Create a plan to regularly 'see,' 'be with' and 'hear' what is happening in your department. Leverage a variety of strategies and communication channels. Consider existing channels and create new ones. Just as you have established a plan to meet regularly with your boss, plan on getting to know and staying in touch with the individuals that report to you. Your team will appreciate the fact that you are focused on each member, and you'll have a team that is more engaged and committed to their work. Ultimately, you want to give the illusion of being present when you are not present. Your team will know you and your expectations and will naturally consider your expectations as they navigate challenges and support one another.

Be deliberate as you create a plan to enhance your visibility.

Consider the following as you create your plan:

- Scheduled time for observing on every shift at some routine interval (spend 2-4 hours on a weekend or night shift monthly)

- Scheduled time to observe patient/staff interactions

- Scheduled time to routinely talk with patients about their care experience

- Formal routine staff meetings (monthly)

- Post open office hours (weekly)

- Process to discuss impromptu concerns with associates in person (when they arise) – some routine presence on all shifts regularly

- Having a meaningful conversation with every associate monthly – this may mean having a phone call to check-in if you miss someone

- Process to capture issues, concerns and themes

- Process and timeline for feedback loop for follow-up

- A log to track and share issues, findings and follow-up

As you juggle your discovery journey, ease into your visibility plan by the third week. Deliberately, evolve it as you navigate through your first 90 days. Plan to have it fully implemented by the end of your first three months. The first goal of your visibility plan is to meet each member of your team. Get to know who they are. As you get to know members of your team, assess their individual and team performance. Assess your team to determine if there is alignment of attitude, skill and ability with the work needing to be accomplished. Ensure the right people are doing the right work. As you create relationships with members of your team, ask and listen. Consider the following questions as you are interacting with team members:

- ✓ **How are they meeting expectations individually and as a team?**

- ✓ **How do they demonstrate they have the skill and ability to complete the work?**

- ✓ **Are the right people doing the right work?**

- ✓ **What experience do they have?**

- ✓ **Who is capable?**

- ✓ **Are they in the right job?**

- ✓ **Do they have the right responsibilities?**

- ✓ **How are they viewed outside of your team?**

- ✓ **What are their aspirations?**

- ✓ **What are they most proud of?**

- ✓ **What are their concerns?**

- ✓ **What are their challenges?**

✓ **What are the obstacles keeping them from succeeding?**

✓ **What are they afraid that you may do?**

Nurse Managers, on average, have 50 direct reports, with some having more than twice that many. This kind of span of control requires becoming a master at prioritizing your schedule. **Who among your team should you get to know first?** I suggest you start with the leaders, both formal and informal. With a department that has operations around the clock, you likely have leaders reporting to you – team leaders, charge nurses, assistant managers, educators and council leaders are individuals who have significant influence over others. In addition, there may be others by nature of their experience or personality that wield influence. Whether in formal leadership roles or informally leading, all of these individuals are an extension of you. **Are they representing you the way you want them to represent you?** Prioritize getting to know these members of your team first. Then, move onto all other members of your team. Balance your interactions among shifts and roles. Make a note of the issues you may hear. Address what you can and follow-up. There may be some quick wins that will give you momentum for things to come. Ask and listen. Limit how much you talk. Listen.

Ideally, you want to help every member of your team achieve more than they ever imagined. Each team member may need something different, so find the themes. In return, your team will do great work. Build a habit of not telling or giving advice. This is an important leadership skill to grow from the beginning. You have much to do. Your goal is to help your team discover answers for themselves whenever possible. Avoid just giving them the answers; teach them to be self-sufficient. This level of leadership is superior to task-management – lead yourself and lead your team as you manage to the expected outcomes. Help people perform at their best.

Manage your availability can be challenging. First, it is okay to have your office door closed occasionally. You will have work to do that you alone can do. Closing your office door and moving through that work uninterrupted will keep you efficient. Ultimately giving you more time with your team. Secondly, be careful about inviting your team to "call anytime." With the immediate availability that exits with our mobile phones, you may quickly become bombarded at all hours of the day. Although you have 24-hour accountability you need time to refresh and refuel. Be transparent with your team regarding your availability. If they know what to expect from your availability, they will interrupt you less. Give them guidelines for when and what kind of issues you want to be notified. Give them guidelines for what constitutes an urgent or emergent call, or what should be managed via email. Provide guidelines as to what your response time will be. Provide guidelines and implement processes so they can make decisions on their own. Share your expectations and empower them to make decisions when you are not there. Ensure that they know you support their choices. Let your team know that you trust them.

Prioritize Your Relationships – I have discussed several key relationships that you will want to develop. I discussed building relationships with your boss, your 'first team,' key medical staff members and your direct reports as a first priority. You also need to evaluate other individuals on the list your created. Of everyone on your list which relationships are most essential. Evaluate the current state of each relationship. Consider the following:

- **Are you acquaintances or strangers?**

- As you change levels in the organizational structure, you may have a previous boss who is now your peer. **How will you get to know them as a peer?**

- **Are there areas that have an adversarial relationship with you or your team?**

- **Who are your greatest supporters?**

- **Who are your team's champions?**

- **Who will you go to for honest and credible feedback?**

Consider how each relationship may need to change and what you need to do to build a meaningful and productive relationship:

- **Are these the people who support you?**

- **What opportunities exist to build stronger support?**

- **Do these relationships need to shift from adversarial to supporter? Casual acquaintance to supporter?**

- **Is there unresolved conflict or history between your department and others that may influence these relationships?**

- Be honest with yourself as well – **What "story" are you bringing into the relationship?**

Next, prioritize these relationships to determine which you need to build first:

- **Who is most critical to your success?**

- **Who is most critical to achieve the outcomes you are looking to achieve?**

- **Which relationships do you need to remedy?**

- **Who will have the most immediate impact on your work?**

- **What will be the ongoing cadence of meetings to maintain a good working relationship?**

- **Is there a cadence for interacting with individuals (or teams) already?** It is likely that there is some cadence of regular team meetings established in the organization – consider how you will leverage these opportunities.

After consideration of the above, create a heat map detailing the goal for each relationship, the importance to your effective leadership and the effort each will require. Use the heat map to determine the cadence for when you plan to meet with them. This will take time, so give yourself an appropriate timeframe. Consider the circle of safety discussed earlier. Each of these relationships is significant to your leadership. Act deliberately, stay curious and bring your authentic self forward.

Grow Collaborative Relationships – You want to build channels for healthy dialogue with the individuals on your list. I have discussed strategies to accomplish this with your boss, the medical staff and your team of direct reports. It is important that as you meet with members of your first team and other individuals on your list, you act with as much intention. Whether you invite them to have lunch with you, have a cup of coffee or meet with them in their office, you want to plan these opportunities to be meaningful and time well spent. Plan a 30-minute session with a clear agenda. Your goal is to build the foundation for a meaningful relationship with open communication that is authentic and honest. In time you will work together to address issues that you both may face. Creating open channels before issues arise will enhance collaboration later. Creating a channel requires listening, deep understanding and mutual appreciation for the work and goals of the other. It is deeper than just communicating. Prepare for your individual meetings with this mindset.

"I believe that you can get everything in life you want if you will just help enough other people get what they want." – Hillary Hinton "Zig" Ziglar, author, motivational speaker

Prepare an agenda for each meeting that is individualized to the person while supporting your learning journey. It will be important that you do more listening than talking. Be inquisitive and ask great questions. Remember, time is a valuable treasure, and you need to make the time valuable for both of you. Give them the chance to share what they think you need to know. This is a crucial first step to creating that meaningful relationship you desire and it will give you extraordinary insights. Be deliberate and share your authentic, genuine desire to learn from each of them. Be careful not to get defensive if you hear something undesirable. Be open and absorb as much as you can. Honor their time. Use the following 7-step plan to help create a meaningful agenda for these sessions:

STEP 1 – Create your agenda – consider how the agenda should be individualized for the leader you are meeting. **What do you already know that may provide some insight into what is important to them?**

STEP 2 – Arrive on time, start with the common courtesies, thank them for taking the time to meet with you, introduce and share a bit about yourself (be brief – this meeting is about them)

STEP 3 – Seek to understand your colleagues' point of view. **What is important for them to be successful? What is important for you to know about your portfolio from this individual's perspective?** Develop 2-3 questions to discuss. Some questions for you to consider:

What are your personal and professional goals? Your department's goals?

What are your greatest challenges?

What do you see as the greatest challenge in your areas of responsibility?

What are the greatest strengths in the department?

What needs to happen to capitalize on our opportunities?

If you were me, what would you focus your attention on?

What do you want to keep, and what do you want to change?

STEP 4 – Ask what they need from you and your team. Consider asking what they are afraid you may do. Let them ask you questions. Discuss how you will communicate moving forward.

STEP 5 – Get advice on who else may be good for you to get to know and who the other influential leaders are that you should have on your radar.

STEP 6 – Close on time and thank them for their time.

STEP 7 – Follow-up. If you made a commitment to anything, do what you said you would do. Send them a follow-up email thanking them for their time. Schedule your next meeting if you agreed to a regular cadence.

This listening journey *will* take time. Growing relationships takes thoughtful planning. Plan for the most essential relationships first. Accomplish what you can in the first 30 or 60 days. This process is ongoing, so work through your list understanding that it will likely take you beyond your first 90 days.

Define

The discovery process has taken you through a review of processes, projects, performance and people. You are discovering a great deal about the culture, organization and your department. You are beginning to see patterns and themes. There is a great deal of learning in all of the notes taken from your conversations, observations and the data you have reviewed. You are forming and testing hypotheses and making assumptions. You have discovered problems that need to be solved, opportunities for processes to improve and for people to grow. You have discovered what areas are fully optimized and which may need to be supported. You have identified problems that need to be resolved immediately, and maybe you have already addressed some.

"Our life is the sum total of all the decisions we make every day, and those decisions are determined by our priorities" – Myles Munroe, minister, author, founder

In the words of Peter Drucker, "management is doing things right, leadership is doing the right things." Your current state analysis is leading you to a treatment plan, leveraging the strengths and resources you discovered. You are becoming aware of what needs to be done, what needs to be managed and where your leadership is most needed. Be cautious about jumping too quickly into solutions. You do want to find the right diagnosis. Between 30 and 60 days, you will want to define your priorities and the initial steps you plan to take. By the end of your first 30 days, begin discussing your leadership priorities. By 60 days, you want clarity on what success looks like for the next six to twelve months, along with a plan for moving forward.

This can be overwhelming. **There is much to learn and much to do, correct?** Take a breath. I want you to pause for a moment. First, healthcare is one of the most complex industries in the world (according to Guru Peter Drucker) and you are leading care delivery. The Nurse Manager role, in my opinion, is one of the most challenging roles in the organization. I imagine you are discovering the many hats you are responsible for wearing and the many balls you are required to juggle. It can be overwhelming. You cannot eat the whole elephant in one bite. Do not try to. You must prioritize everything including the priorities given to you to execute from other levels in the organization. Identify with your boss what is required and what is non-negotiable. Focus on what is most important. Identify where you can find quick wins. Consider the following:

- **What needs to be addressed first?**

- **What skills do you need to master first (financial management? staffing? quality management?)**

- **What quick start tasks will support you managing the business as you learn to master skills?**

- **Where are the quick wins?**

- **What strategies are necessary to tackle those issues?**

- **How can you influence the change that is necessary?**

- **What are the short-term gains for long-term goals?**

- **Are there steps you can take that could address multiple issues in parallel?**

When faced with a to-do list that seems overwhelming, you need to prioritize. Ask your boss and mentor for some guidance here. Be deliberate with your calendar and your time. Take ownership of your responsibilities because you are empowered to take action. You want to be both realistic and aspirational. You want to dedicate time to leading yourself, leading your team and managing the business. Determine the amount of time to spend on the management tasks you need to master and the actions to move your department forward. Start a high-level timeline to address concerns you have discovered.

As you prioritize solutions or actions to address the concerns identified, I suggest using a priority matrix. This tool allows for an objective evaluation of each task or project based on a variety of factors: time, importance, money, manpower and dependence on other accomplishments. With a clear way of charting priorities, this tool can help you determine where to start. It will help you become more productive and efficient. This is a tool that comes from Stephen Covey. It consists of four quadrants organized by effort and impact. Along the x axis (horizontal) is the level of impact. The project is mapped based on the outcomes it is expected to achieve from low to high, left to right. On the y axis (vertical) is effort. The project is mapped based on resources needed (degree of change required, time, money) from low to high, top to bottom. With each of your ideas mapped against the impact and effort axis using you will end up with a scatter diagram. Divide the map with a vertical and horizontal line making four equal squares. Your priorities are now divided into four categories – "Quick Wins" that have high impact and low effort, "Major Projects" with high impact and high effort, "Fill In's" with low impact and low effort and "Thankless Tasks" with low impact and high effort. See the figure below.

Figure: Priority Matrix

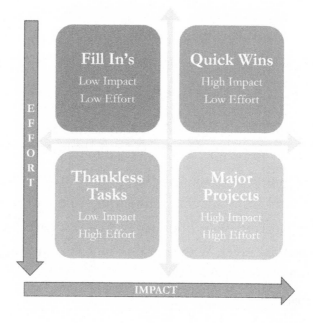

Let's take a deeper look at each quadrant:

- *Quick Wins* (high impact, low effort) – These are high-value projects. They may have been previously unforeseen or procrastinated. You should consider these critical or urgent.

  LEADER ACTION: Do these first.

- *Major Projects* (high impact, high effort) – These are high-value projects that are more complicated to execute. These tasks will yield a high impact in the long run. They are often neglected or not prioritized due to the effort required.

  LEADER ACTION: Establish a timeline with clear interim goals and build in checkpoints.

- *Fill-Ins* (low impact, low effort) – These are less important projects. They can be delegated and deprioritized.

  LEADER ACTION: Delegate or do not do.

- *Thankless Tasks* (low impact, high effort) – These projects have little impact and are time-consuming. They can be distractions.

  LEADER ACTION: Avoid these if possible.

Ideally, your list would be of full "quick win" projects. In reality, this is not likely to be true. You will need to juggle projects in each quadrant – projects that are easy and quick to address and projects with short term gains for long term wins. The tool is helpful in guiding you to clarify your priorities so that you make the most of your time and resources. With your priority matrix in hand, it is time for you to declare your leadership priorities and share them to get some feedback.

If you think about this in terms of your nursing practice, you have done your analysis of assessment findings, collaborated with other members of the healthcare team and formed your diagnoses. Before implementing a treatment plan, you would share your findings with your patient. You would gain agreement on the goals and then you would determine the appropriate steps to take. Similarly, it is time for you to declare your priorities and begin the process of negotiating these with key stakeholders – your boss, direct reports and others who will be impacted by your actions. This is a time to be resolute, empowered, and deliberate. Stay inquisitive about what you may not see, what else you might discover and how you want to address concerns. You want to leverage the relationships you are forming and the management tools you are learning to move forward.

I have mentioned Michael Watkins's book, *The First 90 Days*, as a resource for transitions. In his book, he details the steps to take and things to consider as you prioritize your actions. Most importantly, he stresses fostering a strong relationship with your boss. I discussed your boss relationship previously, in the discussion about people. I am stressing it again here to ensure you are fully aware and in synch with your boss's expectations. You want to fully embrace your boss's accountabilities and understand your boss's pressures. Make sure your boss understands your assessment and is aligned with your diagnoses. Through ongoing conversations, let your boss know that you will be coming back with a more detailed goal and action plan before moving forward. Agree on a timeline. You may discuss some of your initial ideas regarding the specifics, but do not leave your team and others out of the planning. Be deliberate in getting the feedback you need. Keeping others engaged in the goal setting and planning process will support alignment and the execution yet to come. These are critical conversations you should be having with your team and colleagues, as you negotiate with the stakeholders along the way.

Navigating through the discover and "define" leg of your journey will help you find clarity on your purpose. You will experience a deeper understanding of your level of authority and that which you own. You've started to share more of yourself. You have intentionally begun to build strong relationships and have methodically reviewed processes and performance. You asked too many questions to count and listened wholeheartedly to answers. You have been inquisitive and curious about the deeper meaning behind what has been shared. You created priorities to tackle. You are sharing your light and beginning to inspire that light in those around you. You are *READI* for the next leg in your journey – to build a plan to lead your department someplace new.

"When you are clearly-defined, deliberate with intention and operating at your highest level, your brilliance cannot be hidden, diminished or overshadowed." – Rhonda Louise Robbins, certified life coach

30 Days: Discover & Define

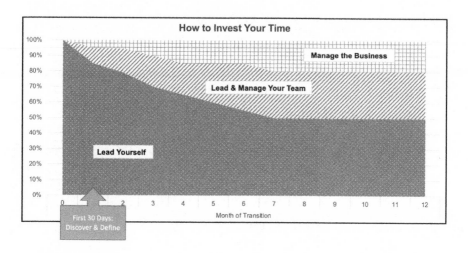

Actions to take:

✓ Find a mentor – negotiate frequency for regular check-ins and how to connect when issues pop-up

✓ Seek out the management tools, resources and classes that your company offers

✓ Complete assessment using checklist - processes, projects, performance

✓ Make a list of the processes you want to learn and establish a timeline to learn the processes identified

✓ Add to your journal – take notes on what you discover, identify themes and list your assumptions and questions

✓ Clarify communication expectations with your boss

✓ Identify your boss's pressures and goals

✓ Develop your leadership visibility plan then follow it

✓ Create a plan to meet with key medical staff members

✓ Identify key relationships and complete a relationship heat map to sequence, build and manage these key relationships

✓ Manage your calendar:

  – Schedule routine check-ins with your boss

  – Schedule routine check-ins with your mentor

  – Schedule time for observations

  – Schedule agreed upon training classes

  – Schedule key deadlines with work time

  – Ensure all team meetings are on your calendar

  – Schedule 1:1 meetings with key individuals identified

  – Schedule time based on visibility plan

✓ Identify key initiatives and complete a priority matrix

✓ Define the quick wins

✓ Create a draft timeline to address priorities identified

Tools Shared

✓ Checklists for discovery of process, projects and performance

✓ Key stakeholder checklist

✓ Boss Relationship Dos & Don'ts

✓ Relationship Heat Map

✓ 7-step plan for 1:1 sessions with colleagues

✓ Visibility Plan

✓ Priority Matrix

Quick hints as you start managing the business:

✓ Hearing from the patients directly and observing patient interactions will go a long way in understanding and improving care delivered by your department.

✓ An FTE (full time equivalent) works 40 hours in a week and 2,080 in a year. FTE's are used to determine the number of positions you fill and the labor budget you are responsible to manage. The number of FTEs you have is different than the number of people you need to have hired. For example, 10 FTEs may be 7 individuals working 40 hours/week and 6 people working 20 hours/week. In this example, 10 FTEs means 13 people. Determine how many FTEs you have, how many associates you have hired and the positions that need to be filled. Clarify this with your boss.

✓ An HPPD (hour per patient day) is the number of hours worked in a day in your department, divided by the number of admitted patients at a designated time, usually by midnight. HPPD is used to determine the FTE's variable to volumes of patients and is used to compare labor resources across departments. Determine your target HPPD and clarify this with your boss.

CHAPTER FIVE
60 Days: PLAN

"Every minute you spend in planning saves 10 minutes in execution; this gives you a 1,000 percent return on energy!" – Brian Tracy, author & motivational speaker

You have navigated through your first month. You are learning and learning some more. You are learning new processes, learning tasks you need to complete and learning about your leadership.

You are learning more about the role and responsibilities to manage the business and lead your team. You are learning about challenges you need to solve and processes you need to implement.

You've gained agreement on your initial leadership priorities; you've gained clarity on what success looks like. Keep your spirit of inquiry while you refine your initial goals. Create a plan balancing directives from the organization and your own desires to move the department forward. Your focus remains on leading yourself as you begin investing more time in leading your team and managing initial business processes. Stay resolute in your purpose, you are empowered to do the right things, share your aspirations by bringing your authentic self to your interactions, remain deliberate and inquisitive. Get *READI* to plan.

This may go without needing to be said – I am going to say it anyway. Planning is a critical step. Far too often in the excitement and haste of wanting to "fix" a problem or in the sight of an overwhelming amount of responsibility, leaders fail to adequately plan. When this happens, those same leaders are faced with further stress, frustration and even bigger problems. I am raising the caution flag. Failing to plan is planning to fail. Stay deliberate about the actions you take. Planning provides the foundation for managerial action by articulating the objectives and the means to achieve them. Planning is deliberate and systematic. Planning is future oriented, looking ahead and preparing for both challenges and opportunities. Planning requires consideration of both internal and external environmental factors facing your department and organization. All that said, you will be expected to take action. Do not get stuck in planning for perfection. You will not be effective if you wait for "the perfect plan." Leadership and planning are not perfect. Winston Churchill, former British Prime Minister said, "Plans are of little importance, but planning is essential." It is less about the plan than the ongoing process of planning. Florence Nightingale said, "Everything is sketchy. The world does nothing but sketch," implying that all plans are incomplete. Any plan you make will need to change as you learn more. Become comfortable with 'good enough' or 'done enough'. Do not get too attached to creating a perfect plan. Be cautious of getting too attached to your plan. Be resolute in your overarching goals and flexible in your plan so that you can shift when needed. Planning involves choice. It is the process of choosing among alternative pathways. It is continuous and ongoing. To help you successfully lead through this planning process, I will share a few lessons, tools and models. I will review goal setting and leveraging resources. I will provide a brief overview of quality management and change leadership. My goal in sharing these principles is to help you develop fruitful plans and grow your planning discipline as a leader.

"So be sure when you step, step with care and great tact. And remember that life's a great balancing act. And will you succeed? Yes! You will, indeed!" –
Theodor Seuss Geisel, Dr. Suess

As a leader, you need to strike the right balance between planning, trying, rethinking and trying again. The problems you are facing will determine the time spent planning, and the risk or consequences will determine how much planning needs to be done before implementing. As deliberate as you are in your nursing practice, is how deliberate your should be in planning. Always start with the destination in mind (your goal). Your plan needs to get you there. Consider the root cause of the challenges you are facing – the strengths, weaknesses, opportunities and threats. Consider your key priorities and quick wins. Our nursing practice includes collaborating with other disciplines to coordinate the care of our patients, ensuring that the strategy matches the diagnoses to achieve the desired outcome. Similarly, you will work with others to refine your goals, then develop and implement your plan of attack. Engage with your team and colleagues as you establish and refine your goals. Work with the appropriate stakeholders as you develop your action plan. What you accomplish and how it is accomplished will define your success. Bringing others along with you will enable that success.

Set Goals

"The trouble with not having a goal is that you can spend your life running up and down the field and never score." – Bill Copeland, author, poet, historian

Planning starts with a goal. Without a goal, you will lack direction. As you take action, you need a clear vision of what you are trying to accomplish. You want clarity in your aim. Clearly defined goals provide focus, guidance, and direction while serving to inspire and motivate. Clearly defined goals can also serve as a way to evaluate and control performance. Goals can help you achieve more. Tony Robbins, author of *Awaken the Giant Within,* said, "Setting goals is the first step in turning the invisible into the visible." Clearly defined goals will make what you desire visible to yourself and others. I like to use the acronym SMART to help provide that visibility. Goals that are specific, measurable, achievable, relevant and time-bound (SMART) are clear and visible.

SMART goals should be focused on people, processes and strategy.

- Specific – The goal should be clear and highly specific. You should be able to see it.

- Measurable – You need to be able to accurately track your progress and judge if the goal has been met.

- Attainable – The goal should be ambitious, yet within reach. You want it to be a challenge but defined enough to achieve it.

- Relevant – Your goal should be pertinent, purposeful and benefit you, your team and department directly.

- Time-Bound – The goal should have a defined timeframe and a target date for accomplishment.

Work with your team and colleagues to create and refine your goals. This is a great way to build and support engagement. Use the development of SMART goals to motivate your team to take action. Once goals are established, you have the foundation on which to build your plan. Continuing to involve others as plans are developed will promote buy-in. Creating your plan with this collaborative spirit, soliciting feedback, socializing plans and gaining consensus will enable your *READI* leadership.

Build Your Plan

Your organization is likely to have an action plan template they support. You may have one that you are already familiar with using. You can also find options available online. Regardless of the template you use, the key components of an action plan include:

- The problem you are trying to solve

- The goal (that is SMART) you want to achieve

- The individual action steps

    - To be completed by whom?

    - To be completed by when?

    - Resources available/needed

    - Potential barriers

    - Stakeholders

- Communication that needs to occur to whom and by whom

- Process to track progress

> *"It does not do to leave a live dragon out of your calculations, if you live near one."* – J.R.R. Tolkien, the Hobbit

To complete the plan, think of anything and everything you and your team need to accomplish in order to achieve your SMART goal. Make a list. Engage team members (as appropriate) to help make that list. Identify the obstacles you need to overcome. Identify the risks and resources needed. Identify skill and knowledge gaps that may exist. Identify the strategies to overcome gaps. Identify the people and resources that you can solicit to help. Consider *all* contingencies. The more complete the list, the better your plan. The better the plan, the more effective you and your team will be.

Through their research Joseph Grenny, Kerry Patterson, David Maxfield, Ron McMillan and Al Switzler share insights of behavioral scientists and leaders as they tell stories of incredible change in their book, *Influencer: The New Science of Leading Change*. (Another for your must-have list.) They believe in order to influence change; we must first be specific about what we are trying to change. They suggest identifying the "crucial moments" where decisions are made and then determine the "vital behaviors" that will drive the new behavior. Their research shows deliberate focus on changing these high-leverage, vital behaviors in the crucial moment, any problem – big or small – can be solved. In addition, Grenny and his colleagues identified six sources of influence that support sustained change. They discuss these six sources in a table with two drivers – motivation and ability and in three areas – personal, social and structural. The authors advise addressing as many of the six sources as possible to improve the likelihood of adherence to new behaviors. In my own experience I've found that addressing at least four of the six is effective. The six sources are:

- *Personal Motivation* – This source addresses individuals desire to change. It involves an individual decision regarding effort and reward. Does the new vital behavior itself bring people enough incentive for their effort? If not, how can you get people (yourself or others) to do things they currently find undesirable?

  LEADER ACTION – Consciously connect to values. Help individuals find their personal source of motivation.

- *Personal Ability* – This source focuses on the need to learn and practice in order to master the new behavior. It addresses the knowledge skill and physical capability to perform. It necessitates the ability to manage the personal emotion and resistance associated with the behavior change.

  LEADER ACTION – Invest in the right training for skill building and demand deliberate practice. Provide feedback and allow time for debriefing.

- *Social Motivation* – Otherwise known as peer pressure, this source focuses on the social network. This includes peer expectations, social rewards and collective consequences. Are others encouraging the right behavior and discouraging the wrong behavior?

  LEADER ACTION – Model the way. Enlist informal leaders to champion the new behavior. Leverage those individuals who enable and encourage others. Harness peer pressure.

- *Social Ability* – Similar to social motivation, this source focuses on the social network and the willingness for individuals to offer support and aid to one another in order to successfully implement the change. The group can produce a force greater than the sum of individual efforts. When used properly, it is this help or "social capital" that enables new norms to be formed.

LEADER ACTION – Model the way. Enlist informal leaders to champion the new behavior. Leverage those individuals who enable and encourage others. Find strength in numbers.

- *Structural Motivation* – This source focuses on reward and punishment. This can be tricky. First, rely on personal and social motivators. Processes and rewards must be established that make doing the right thing easy and the wrong thing difficult. Are rewards (pay, promotions, performance reviews, or perks) encouraging the right behaviors and/or discouraging the wrong behaviors?

LEADER ACTION – Identify meaningful rewards and create rewards that are connected to the critical moment and the new vital behavior. Be cautious of rewarding the outcome alone. Demand accountability to the new behavior.

- *Structural Ability* - This source focuses on the environment. The impact of the physical world on human behavior is profound. Alter the environment and alter behavior. Are there enough cues to stay on course? Does the environment (tools, facilities, information, reports, or policies) enable the right behaviors and/or discourage the wrong behaviors?

LEADER ACTION – Use space intentionally. Use data, ques and visual management to direct, remind and encourage. Change the environment.

As you build your plan, address the crucial moments and identify the specific vital new behavior that will support your SMART goal. Apply strategies that address both thoughts (motivation) and actions (ability). Analyze the six sources of influence and deploy tactics that span the sources of influence. With thorough review you will discover where you may find your best leverage and where you might get stuck. Most change efforts fail because of unrealistic expectations and reliance on one simple solution. The more you leverage multiple sources to support the change, the more you set yourself up for success.

Depending on the problem you are trying to solve, your plan may need to be iterative, meaning that you'll be testing steps or testing processes before implementing a large-scale change. In fact, I suggest you consider rapid cycle testing whenever possible. It is often the best way to find the right improvements in the least amount of time. My first exposure to rapid cycle change was from the Institute of Health Care Improvement, (this organization has a wealth of information as you work to improve care delivery) when I was involved in a national collaborative to improve patient safety. It changed my thinking about action planning. Rather than having a fully developed plan and implementing it on a large scale, I learned a new process that allowed my teams to test and learn quickly. It supported more rapid improvements.

The rapid cycle change model, Plan Do Study Act (PDSA), is based in the scientific method and regulates the desire to take immediate action. Once an aim (goal) is identified, the first step is to *plan* – to develop an intervention that is predicted to make an improvement. Outcomes are clearly stated and tasks are assigned. It is in this phase that the, who, what, when, and where of the plan is determined. The second step is *do*, during which the plan is implemented, results are observed and documented. The next step is to *study*. Data is collected and results are studied. The final step of the cycle is *act* – to take an action based on the "study."

Decisions are made to adopt and spread, adapt and test again, or abandon the intervention. PDSA is simple, yet powerful. It supports rapid change in small increments, which allows you and your team to learn and pivot, getting to the outcome more quickly. PDSA cycles create building blocks for iterative improvement. This rapid cycle change is also a great way of engaging your team and encouraging their ownership of solutions. It provides a mechanism for those delivering care to be involved with how to improve it. They can participate during their normal workday, share observations and ideas and ultimately get to see the fruits of their labor. **How can you leverage PDSA cycles to make improvements?** Determine what aspects of your plan may benefit from this iterative process and include it into your planning routine when it fits.

To be thorough in action planning, think about and leverage the resources available to you. Consider the quality management system utilized in your organization and be intentional to incorporate change leadership into the steps. I will share more about each of these subjects on the following pages, while providing some lessons learned, theories and tools to help you identify steps to create a more thorough plan. The content will also enhance your leadership as you execute your plan.

Leverage Your Resources

"You can do anything but not everything." – David Allen, author, productivity expert

During the discovery phase, you learned a great deal about the organization, team, other departments and the resources available to you. Engage them as you plot your course and begin to take steps toward accomplishing the goals established. A common mistake I see leaders all too often make is having a view of leadership that is a lone solitary soul ahead of the pack, pathing a trail, burdening the work alone, achieving glory alone. This thought process is damaging. It is not a view of leadership that works in the environment you are leading. Even if that is not your viewpoint, my guess is you place some degree of pressure on yourself to not want to be perceived as incapable. This too can prevent you from reaching out for help. This is common among nurse leaders, particularly new leaders. Don't let your fear of being judged stop you from asking for help. Ask for help along the way and get others on board with your success

Soliciting help was a difficult lesson for me. A lesson I wish I learned earlier. Although I encouraged others to ask for help, I secretly felt that as a leader, it was my job to help others and not to need help myself. I preferred to give and be seen as someone who serves. In reality, what I was doing was trying to be a lonesome hero to gain that glory. Of course, I gave credit to the team, but I was secretly enjoying being the hero. I told myself a story that I was less than good if I needed assistance. In the meantime, I was working way more hours than necessary, I was not accomplishing as much as I should have. I fell behind. Worse, I was not accepting help when offered, denying others the reward of helping. I learned (the hard way) that I did need help and that others were more than happy to give help. I learned that the act of asking for and accepting help fostered stronger relationships. Together, we achieved the work. Overused humility and overused pride prevented me from asking for help.

"One of the biggest defects in life is the inability to ask for help." – Robert Kiyosaki, author, founder of Rich Dad Company

If we ever think our needs are less worthy than others or we do not want to show our vulnerabilities, we will not ask for the help we need. **Do you readily ask for help? When should you have asked for help but did not?** As humans, we feel good when we help others. Albert Einstein once said, "Strange is our situation here upon earth. Each of us comes for a short visit, not knowing why, yet sometimes seeming to divine a purpose. From the standpoint of daily life, however, there is one thing we do know: that man is here for the sake of other men." We are creatures made for community. Our humanness comes with a desire to help – our DNA is wired this way. We are inspired when we are needed. We actually feel more connected to the people we help. By not asking we rob people of that innate joy of helping. Brene' Brown, research professor at the University of Houston, is a leading expert on courage, vulnerability and shame. She suggests, "Offering help is courageous and compassionate, but so is asking for help." When you start a new position, you are expected to need help, and there is no shame in asking for it. You may need help finding your way, understanding the culture, or navigating through the available resources. I encourage you to be courageous and ask for help. Ask for help to foster strong relationships, to advocate for your team, to get what you need, to reach your goals and inspire others. Build this habit from the start. Your need for help will not stop. You will grow your authenticity. It will empower you.

Checklist Manifesto: How to Get Things Right by Atul Gawande is a great example of a resource to leverage. In this book, Gawande, a general and endocrine surgeon, illustrates that a simple checklist can help to unravel the complexity of care and create consistently safe processes. Care is complex and is only growing in complexity. Care is provided by numerous, exceptionally proficient, and expert clinicians who are human and are impacted by the "life" around them. Even the most expert professionals are challenged to constantly remember every task within every procedure. A simple check list can help. Depending on your clinical background, you may have leveraged checklists in your own practice. They exist today to prevent infections, in surgical suites to ensure all team members are aligned before a procedure, to ensure a safe environment, among many other uses in our healthcare settings. I share this here as you begin creating your plan as a resource to leverage and inspire you. Keeping the patient at the center of what we do, simplicity can often be the solution when integrated into the complexity of necessary processes. It may help you get things right.

Help can come from many places. It can come from your team, your colleagues, your boss, your professional network inside and outside of the organization. Help can come from professional organizations, journals and publications. Leverage all of the resources available to you. Leverage the expertise inside and outside of your organization. Research best practices. Ask your team to research the literature (this is a great professional development tactic). You have access to professional networks. Perhaps colleagues have worked to solve these problems and you can learn from what they have done. Professional organizations, such as ANOL, have social media platforms to enable inquiry across their network. Take advantage of the knowledge that exists. Use all of these resources that are available to you. Leverage your resources to create the plan, use help to execute your plan and enjoy success with everyone.

Use a Quality Management System

"The ideas of control and improvements are often confused with one another. This is because quality control and quality improvement are inseparable." – Karou Ishikawa, organizational theorist & professor

In any business, quality management is important. The stakes are high in healthcare, particularly at the point of care, where you are leading. Strong quality management processes ensure quality care is delivered. I am sure you are discovering that quality is measured in a variety of ways. Quality is measured through processes, outcomes and reliability. Stephen Covey, in his famous book *The 7 Habits of Highly Effective People*, defines effectiveness as "the balance of achieving the outcomes you desire with caring for those who produce those outcomes." As a servant leader, you want to ensure processes are followed and quality outcomes are achieved while showing respect for the people preforming the work. You want to inspire excellence in them to strive for improvements in care. Most organizations utilize a defined and disciplined process to manage quality. Follow your organizations processes. Include your team as much as possible in that process, respecting their knowledge of their workflows and their understanding of their obstacles. Entertain their ideas to remedy the issues. Help them own the problems and the solutions. Empower them. There is abundant research in nursing literature, illustrating that empowerment improves the nurse's work environment and patient outcomes. This research is behind the Structural Empowerment pillar of the American Nurses Credentialing Center's Magnet Framework, which states, "Staff need to be developed, directed, and empowered to find the best way to accomplish the organizational goals and achieve desired outcomes." This requires a deliberate approach and a process that supports your leadership principles.

"I define a leader as anyone who takes responsibility for finding the potential in people and processes, and who has the courage to develop that ..." – Brene Brown, researcher & professor

I am going to take the liberty of a bit of a detour. This detour contains important points to help you successfully lead to improve care delivery. My 'go-to' quality management system is "Lean." This may be controversial among some nurse leaders. I respect that. Lean can conjure up lots of emotions depending on individuals' past experiences based on how Lean principles were executed and how Lean tools were used. Many people equate Lean with cost reduction and position elimination. Indeed, process improvement done through Lean principles (or other quality management systems) can end in cost reductions. Although in healthcare leadership a focus on expenses will be expected, that is not why I bring it up here. Lean is so much more than that. Lean at its core is about empowering and respecting others to continuously improve in order to create more value. Leveraged in the healthcare environment it supports the empowerment of caregivers to create more value in care delivery. Lean asserts that the best people to improve the work are those doing the work – this is consistent with the nursing literature previously mentioned. I often repeat Peter Drucker's quote, "management is doing things right, leadership is doing the right things." There are processes that need to be precisely managed to ensure consistent, safe, quality care. Management without leadership, however, can be hurtful to individuals and harmful to the culture. Using Lean principles, I have learned how to foster the development of my teams while achieving results.

The term "lean" was coined to describe Toyota's business during the late 1980s following research led by Jim Womack. Toyota was studied because of the exceptional customer experience it provided while delivering a quality product at a reasonable price (value). The word "lean" was used in reference to the elimination of waste. Have you ever wanted to eliminate a step that did not make sense or stop doing something that did not create value? William Edward Deming, an engineer, statistician and business consultant is broadly acknowledged as a leading quality management expert. His theory teaches that by adopting appropriate principles of management, organizations can increase quality and simultaneously reduce costs. Deming suggests that the aim of leadership is to improve the performance of both people and process, to improve quality, to improve productivity and efficiency, all while encouraging the heart of people and bringing pride of workmanship to people. Deming helped Japan recover from the devastation the country experienced during World War II. Toyota significantly benefited from Deming's work. Ultimately, what we know about Lean is the result of Deming's work.

"It would be better if everyone worked together as a system, with the aim for everybody to win." – Dr. W. Edwards Deming, engineer, statistician & consultant

Deming and Lean both refer to the essential ingredient of respect for people doing the work. This does not mean people won't have to change, on the contrary. It simply means they are respected for the work they do and engaged in the solutions to improve their work. All with the intent to create a better product or experience. Servant leadership calls for us to understand the frustrations of our teams, hear their challenges and help to resolve their concerns. *The Leadership Challenge* identifies leadership behaviors that include challenging processes and enabling others to act. Both suggest that involving the team while leading through improvements is part of exceptional leadership. The second of the two Lean fundamentals is to improve processes to create value. The approach to improve processes focuses on finding and eliminating waste. Eliminating waste in processes improves efficiency and reduces frustration. Improvement is rooted in the scientific method. It requires a clear definition of the problem, understanding the root cause of the problem, establishing a target condition, experimenting, understanding defects, developing countermeasures, seeing the countermeasures through, monitoring both results and processes and standardizing successful processes. Deming's quality management theory and Lean provide a disciplined and deliberate process to ensure that the final process designed will achieve consistent results.

Lean Thinking by Jim Womack and Daniel Jones is a resource that I have used over the years. The book is dog-eared from concepts that I have concentrated on at different times. The authors share several tools that have helped me develop tactics to address issues and lead through the execution of action plans. Lean has been used in healthcare since the late 1990s and early 2000s. There have been mixed results with inconsistent adoption throughout the healthcare industry. John Toussaint, M.D. in his book, *On the Mend: Revolutionizing Healthcare to Save Lives and Transform the Industry,* suggests that lean healthcare is urgently needed and achievable. He asserts that in the complex healthcare delivery system, patients should be able to expect more consistency in outcomes. He asserts that Lean provides solutions to accomplish just that. The authors share real life examples of winning results following Lean principles. Although success in healthcare has been mixed, the disciplined and deliberate approach that Lean provides has merit. Personally, I have used Lean principles and methods to solve many problems, both big and small. Engaging my team, leading them through the systematic approach and utilizing the tools, gave us the ability to achieve numerous, positive outcomes. From improving restraint utilization and decreasing the fall rate, to ensuring that all associates were able to get lunch regularly and consistent onboarding of new employees to reducing shift lengths, Lean has helped me resolve challenges by sharing ownership of problems and their solutions with my team.

"The importance of the quality of management is equal to the management of quality." – Unknown

My reason for this brief detour is to stress the point of using a disciplined, deliberate process to be both methodical in your improvement efforts and to respect the people doing the work. Whatever the management system in your organization, leverage the resources you have, use the tools that are at your disposal, and be deliberate about respecting people in your relentless pursuit to improve outcomes. An improvement plan that creates value without respecting people is harmful to the culture of your department. Be *READI.* What you are managing to and how you are leading to achieve it are vital to your success.

Another commercial – if you want to learn more about Lean, take a look at the Lean Enterprise Institute website. There is a wealth of information available and you are likely to find a tool that will help you create a plan to solve any issues that you may have.

Lead Through Change

"The comfort zone is a nice place, but nothing grows there." — Caroline Cummings, founder Varo Ventures, coach to entrepreneurs

Your role as Nurse Manager requires you to lead your team someplace new. Whether the change is related to continuous improvement or significant organizational strategy, whether it is related to initiatives you and your team create or comes from the direction of others, change is inevitable. Change pushes people out of their comfort zone and creates turmoil. Leadership through the rough waters of change and your willingness to courageously face these challenges with compassion, collaboration, and focus is what the organization needs from you, in your role as Nurse Manager. Change leadership is an essential ingredient to your success. There are a few key points that will help you develop and then execute your plans. I will review theory to provide some context and offer a few tools to support your leadership – to help you to be bold and resolute in your purpose, empowered to do what is right, authentic and aware of your own feelings, deliberate about the steps you will take and inquisitive, curious about the future for your team. Get *READI* to lead through change.

Change is a Process – My first introduction to change theory came during my undergraduate nursing theory class. We reviewed Kurt Lewin's three-stage model: unfreezing, change and refreezing. Lewin's greatest contribution remains the concept of change as a process. His model creates a visual that is easily understood. In order to change, individuals need to unfreeze them from their current state or mindset. Next, they need to work through the confusion, learn and make the change. Finally, they need to refreeze to the new mindset and return to a level of comfort. Lewin's work dates back to the 1940's and although much has been learned about the process of successful change since, leading change as a process holds true. Your job as leader is to lead yourself and others through the process.

Inspire a Vision of a Better Future – According to John Kotter, "Change management refers to a set of tools or structure intended to keep any change effort under control. Change leadership, on the other hand, concerns the driving forces, visions, and processes that fuel transformation." Kotter asserts that management is important, but successful change comes from exquisite leadership versus tactical management alone. John Kotter's research suggests that connecting with people's feelings elicits emotions. It is emotions that facilitate commitment to a behavior change and it is emotions that reinforce behavior once it is changed. In the *Heart of Change*, Kotter introduced the "See-Feel-Change" pattern associated with successful transformation. He states, "people change what they do less because they are given analysis that shifts their thinking than because they are shown a truth that influences their feelings." Emotions activate individuals to change and emotions support ongoing commitment to sustain change. Creating a future that positively connects to emotions will support change.

Daryl Conner further described how emotion can play a significant role in change activation. He introduced the burning platform metaphor in his book, *Managing at the Speed of Change*. He describes how survivors of a catastrophic explosion made the difficult decision to jump into ice-cold water versus staying on the burning platform of the oil-drilling rig. Conner describes how crew members jumped for the chance to survive instead of staying on the platform, facing certain death. They did not jump because there was 100% confidence they would survive. They saw a "truth" that influenced their feelings. They jumped because the fear of staying on the platform was greater than that of jumping. Difficult change is more likely to occur when it is too difficult to stay where you are. Lead through change by making the "comfort zone" of the status quo uncomfortable – create your own burning platform. Successful change leadership requires helping people think and feel differently. It requires focusing on both the head and heart to get the hands engaged in the new behavior expected.

Lead Through Resistance – In *Our Iceberg is Melting* by John Kotter and co-author Holger Rathgeber, they tell a story about a colony of penguins that speaks to the natural resistance that occurs with change. The penguins in the story illustrate the many types of resistance that occurs with change. It offers an inspiring model to follow as people work through change. People are creatures of comfort who seek homeostasis. Resistance is natural. It is a part of change and should be deliberately navigated. All change has an emotional response and leaders often underestimate the emotional response to change. Emotions can be messy. The point is not whether people will have "negative" emotions or not; the point is how you lead through the emotions that will exist. If you fail to make space for these emotions, sabotage will occur. Resistance will still be there, but you will not know of the emotions feeding it. Feelings of fear, anger, grief, confusion, sadness and enthusiasm are common. Finding ways to acknowledge others' emotions will go a long way towards helping them accept and commit to new expectations. Build tactics into your plan to support this reality.

Be Mindful – Be honest with yourself. I have heard many leaders say "I love change" or "Change does not bother me, bring it on!" It is not that I think they were telling falsehoods, just that there are no absolutes. No one loves all change. Although as humans we have an incredible capacity to adapt, we seek stability and homeostasis. Your awareness of your own response to change is critical to your leadership. This is particularly true when you are leading change based on the decisions of others. Do not ignore the feelings that you have about the change you are expected to lead but did not choose. As an agent of the organization, you will be expected to lead your team to accomplish the change. There will be times when you need to work through your own resistance in order to champion the change you are expected to lead. Change is rarely bad; it is just different. Ask yourself, **what is my primary emotion associated with this change? Is it fear, anger or frustration?** Once you identify the emotion, consider what might be feeding this emotion. Ask yourself, **what do I believe to be true that is making me angry/fearful/ frustrated?** This type of questioning will illuminate your own stories that are driving your emotions and influencing your perceptions. This honesty will enable you to be authentic with your team. It will help you connect with others who may be experiencing the same emotions. You will be able to share your own journey to acceptance.

"The only way to make sense out of change is to plunge into it, move with it, and join the dance." – Alan Watts, philosopher & speaker

Provide Support – I would be remiss if I did not discuss Kubler-Ross' change model. Elizabeth Kubler-Ross identified the consistency in emotions observed through change in her groundbreaking work with terminally ill patients. Her model describes the internal, emotional journey that individuals experience when dealing with change. She asserts that change comes with loss and the emotions of loss are similar to the emotions of grief. Kubler-Ross' model identifies the five stages reflective of these emotions. The stages are: denial, anger, bargaining, depression and acceptance. Her model focuses on the individual, emotional journey through change adoption. She emphasizes, that by understanding the five stages of grief, leaders can anticipate reactions and apply appropriate measures to support their team members. Change is a unique and individual experience. It is crucial to know your team and anticipate their reactions so that you are prepared for how these reactions may impact others on the team. Keep an open space for dialogue. Deliberately create a process for them to share so they can support one another and you can support them.

The Change Curve model illustrated below reflects emotion and performance against time. It is broken down into three stages: Endings, Transitions and New Beginnings. It also gives suggestions as to how leaders can support individuals on their specific journey. Understanding the emotional experience illustrated on the curve can help you lead yourself and your team through the dynamic change process. This tool has been successfully used as a mechanism to create safety and openness to discuss personal resistance. Use it for individual discussions or share it during team meetings. Post it in a break room and let individuals map themselves. Your team will feel supported when they realize that their feelings are heard, are natural and are normal. They will feel less alone as they see and hear how their peers are feeling. Team members will help one another. This provides a means for support and encouragement as the team moves forward over time. Your leadership support will help the members of your team progress toward change acceptance and adoption.

Figure: Change Curve

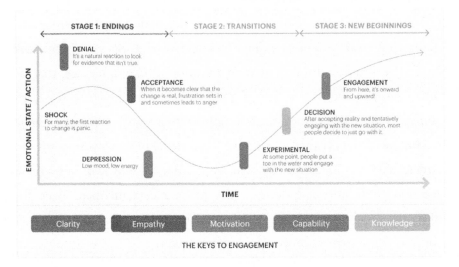

©2017 Mosswarner

"Stand fast in the face of adversity, remaining determined and focused in the quest for the desired goal" – Daryl Conner, author, researcher, organizational change expert

As discussed, a significant part of your responsibility as a leader is to build and sustain a commitment for change. Through his research, Daryl Connor describes three stages of change commitment: preparation, acceptance and commitment. His "Stages of Commitment Model" is the second tool that I encourage you to use. It illustrates the progression of commitment over time. The model also illustrates what happens when commitment is threatened. The goal of your leadership is to keep your team progressing, on the commitment curve, moving toward adoption and reinforcing the need to keep space for dialogue. Keep everyone openly talking about how the change is affecting them and support their progress toward adoption. Humbly inquire about what they are thinking, what is challenging them and what they may need from you. Keeping them in dialogue will support their progress on the change curve and will promote their commitment.

Figure: Stages of Commitment

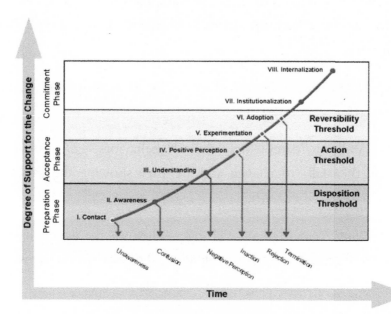

© 2011 ConnerPartners

"When you meet people where they are,
you can take them where they need to be." – Unknown

One last tool that I find essential to the change leadership toolbox is ADKAR. ADKAR was developed by Jeff Hiatt, the founder of Prosci. This model is based on more than 20 years of research. I admire the practicality of the tool, with the basic understanding that organizations do not change unless its people change. ADKAR is an acronym that will help you create tactics to enable your team's successful adoption of change.

- A= Awareness of the need to change – Are associates aware of expectations and do they know what needs to change?

- D= Desire to support the change – How will you inspire the desire to change? What is the burning platform to elicit change? Do associates have the desire to change and support others in changing?

- K= Knowledge of how to change – Do associates know how to change?

- A= Ability to demonstrate skills & behaviors – Do associates have the skills to change and are they showing the expected behaviors?

- R= Reinforcement to make change – How will the right behaviors be reinforced? How can you eliminate the ability to do the wrong thing, making the new process the easy choice?

"Powerful and sustained change requires constant communication, not only throughout the rollout but after the major elements of the plan are in place. The more kinds of communication employed, the more effective they are." –
DeAnne Aguirre, strategy & change consultant

Use ADKAR to help refine your action plan.

Leading through change can be like one of those marble games, where the goal is to get the marbles into the winning space. The challenge is to balance the marbles as you guide them through a maze full of holes and other obstacles. Leading through change is a balancing act. You need to balance the timeline, each element's interdependencies, and the emotional responses that will present themselves. Galvanizing your team around the goal and engaging them to develop the steps to get to the destination will help with commitment and adoption. Keeping the lines of communication open and showing empathy as you maintain expectations are crucial in supporting your team. Use your *READI* leadership to lead your team through change. Be resolute in your vision of a positive future, your expectations and your support for your team as they navigate through it. Take ownership of the change expected, you are empowered to lead. Be authentic, connect with your team through your own values and experiences. Deliberately make space to encourage them to share, show empathy and help them overcome their obstacles. Be inquisitive, ask genuinely to keep them sharing, get curious about how they can help themselves.

"As dealing with change becomes a regular activity, leading it becomes a skill to hone, an internal capacity to master." – Arnaud Henneville, business developer, entrepreneur, author

Wrap-Up Your Plan

In reality, planning never stops but at some point, you do need to move onto the next step. Once you have a complete list of steps, evaluate the interdependencies and timing. Begin to sequence each item. You may discover additional items that you need to add to your list. Combine all of these things into an organized step-by-step plan. Determine who is responsible for each step and when it should be completed. Determine the process you will use to monitor the progress of each step. Some steps may take more time or overlap with other steps. You may discover incremental goals that need to be tracked along the way. Remember, your plan should stay flexible enough to achieve your ultimate goal. With your plan in hand, you are *READI* to begin and take action.

Planning and executing have a symbiotic relationship. As a leader, you are constantly executing your leadership, evaluating and planning your next step. It is nearly impossible to clearly define the end to planning and the beginning of the implementation phase as a leader. The previous discussions about sources of influence, rapid cycle change, leveraging your resources, utilizing a disciplined quality management system and change leadership should provide guidance as you develop your plans. These same concepts provide guidance to help you execute your plans. In the next section, as you approach your 90 days in the role, I will dive deeper into leadership execution. You will notice that as you execute your plan you will further refine your plan.

As you enter into the next leg of your journey, you will demonstrate your purpose with more clarity. You will leverage your authority and illustrate your own empowerment, while working to empower others. Your authentic leadership will enlist followers and earn their trust. Your deliberate actions to establish your goals and then accomplish them will enable successful execution. Your inquiring spirit will support ongoing refinement as you lead forward. *READI* to lead and implement you plans.

60 Days: Plan

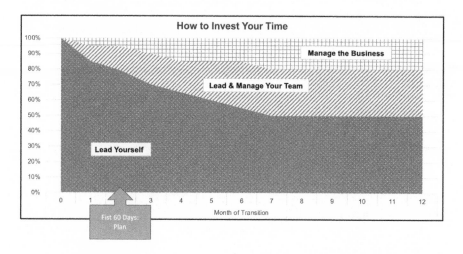

Actions to take:

✓ Manage your calendar

    – Further deploy your visibility plan

    – Continue to progress through your relationship heat map

    – Continue to check off the processes that you are learning and doing independently

✓ Establish SMART goals

✓ Identify risk factors

✓ Inventory the resources available to you

✓ Identify specifics steps leveraging your professional networks and resources inside and outside the organization

✓ Research best practices

✓ Identify resources needed

✓ Integrate rapid cycle change into plan

✓ Use a quality management system and tools to stay disciplined, solution focused and organized

✓ Incorporate steps to manage and lead change into plan

Tools Shared

✓ SMART Goals

✓ Action Plan Components

✓ Rapid Cycle Change Model

✓ Change Curve

✓ Stages of Commitment

✓ ADKAR

Must have for your library:

✓ *Influencer: The New Science of Leading Change, Second Edition* by Joseph Grenny, Kerry Patterson, David Maxfield, Ron McMillan and Al Switzler – the insights will help you build solid processes to improve care delivery

Quick tip hints for success:

✓ Go to the Lean Enterprise Institute website: https://www.lean.org/ and explore the resources available for you.

✓ Do some self-reflection and check your own resistance to changes. Do the self-work to lead effectively.

✓ Gain agreement on the problem before discussing solutions. With agreement, work through the solutions.

✓ Ask patients to share what they notice about care delivery, (keep your questions open ended) inquire further and dig until you fully understand their point of view

✓ Ensure you have the right number of positions to appropriately staff your department. Work with your boss and colleagues from human resources to get positions filled.

CHAPTER SIX
90 Days: Align & Execute

"Ultimately, leadership is not about glorious crowning acts. It's about keeping your team focused on a goal and motivated to do their best to achieve it, especially when the stakes are high and the consequences really matter. It is about laying the groundwork for others' success, and then standing back and letting them shine." – Chris Hadfield, astronaut & commander of the International Space Station

It is time to use your leadership chops to get your team and other key stakeholders on board to execute on the vision of the future you see. Your leadership success obviously relies on what you accomplish. Your success is also dependent on "how" you work to accomplish those goals. Stay *READI*. You prioritized your findings and you negotiated what success looks like. You are empowered to take action. You are getting to know the people that make up the organization and they are getting to know you. Use your vulnerability wisely and be authentic as your build followership. You have been intentional with each step, so remain deliberate in your actions. You were curious, investigated processes, evaluated performances and asked numerous questions. Keep the learning mindset and stay inquisitive. In the previous section, I discussed several topics that can support you throughout your leadership career. Leveraging your resources, staying disciplined with a quality management system and intentional about change leadership will enable your ongoing success. Keep in mind the earlier discussions about the characteristics of a servant leader and the behaviors of exceptional leaders as you take the next steps. You are beginning to invest more time in managing the business and leading your team. Stay deliberate leading yourself as you focus on "how" you accomplish "what" you want to accomplish. Align your team, build a coalition and begin to execute your strategy. Your *READI* leadership will help you create the culture in your department that will lead to great things.

Align Your Team

Remember the brief discussion about culture, and how culture eats strategy from chapter four. Effectively leading your team requires creating a culture in your department where team members are aligned around the organization's mission and with your vision and expectations. Aligning your team around the goals, the strategy and new processes will require strong and thoughtful leadership. You will be making waves. You will be asking your team to make changes. Be intentional about the waves – the timing, the impact and the goals of each. Balance the disruption, sequence changes with the cultural tolerance to keep your team with you. You are getting to know your team, their strengths and desires. You want to help them grow as you work together to accomplish the goals identified. You want to leverage their skills and abilities to the greatest extent possible. I will discuss a few critical components to help you align your team, by communicating your vision and expectations, fostering a collaborative environment, empowering all individuals that make up your team and managing the talent of your team.

Communicate Your Vision and Expectations

"The art of communication is the language of leadership." – James Humes, presidential speech writer

As Kouzes and Posner suggest, you will be at your best and executing well if you follow the five principles they outline in *The Leadership Challenge*. Aligning your team starts with sharing your vision and your expectations. This will help to get others activated. They need to clearly understand your expectations for performance as well as the benefits experienced through these expectations and the consequences that will come with failure to meet them. Create a compelling vision. Help them see the future by creating an ideal and unique image of what could be. Communicate your vision with passion and make it evident that you believe your plans will make a difference. Be authentic – use your personal style and presence to enlist others in your dreams, and get them excited about your vision.

Help you team to feel integral to the plan. Help them imagine a new future. Quick visioning exercises can be useful. With the goal in mind, work with your team to complete this sentence: *Imagine if….* For example, if you are working on a fall prevention strategy that requires your team to implement a new process – have them explore their imagination if they were successful eliminating falls. (You may need to give them examples – *Imagine if* we were able to celebrate zero patient falls after 30 and 60 days. *Imagine if* no patient was ever injured because of a fall. *Imagine if* you never had to complete a post fall assessment, call a physician, schedule an emergency CT scan. *Imagine if* you never had to call a family member because their loved one fell.) Your audience needs to see the passion and excitement about what you are sharing and about what they are imagining. You are creating that burning platform.

Along with a compelling future, your team also needs to feel that you understand the impact of the change to their routines. They need to trust you will support them as they work through it. After sharing your compelling future, ask them what they like and what concerns they may have. In his book, *The Five Dysfunctions of a Team*, Patrick Lencioni said, "It's as simple as this, when people don't unload their opinions and feel like they've been listened to, they won't really get on board." Get your team members to talk about both the benefits and challenges. Use the materials discussed to help navigate. Be authentic and deliberate in your messaging. Stay resolute in your purpose, provide clarity in your expectation and, inquire about their concerns. Effective communication is essential to helping and supporting your team as they manage their own behavior.

"Communicate unto the other person that which you would want him to communicate unto you if your positions were reversed." – Aaron Goldman, author, marketing consultant

Effective communication will lead to understanding. Effective communication requires preparation and an understanding of the audience. Communication is a two-way street. It includes both sending and receiving – sending and receiving are equally important. In fact, according to Patrick Ropella, a global talent management expert, "To achieve great results, frontline leaders must master three essential components of communication: sending communications, receiving communications and giving effective feedback." You must send the right message in a way that can be heard, hear the response and then respond with the right feedback. To effectively communicate starts with organizing your message and preparing for communication that will accomplish these three components. For high stakes messaging, I use a tool to help organize my thoughts to achieve more effective communication. This tool comes from Strathman Associates – coaches who have helped me develop my own authentic leadership. This relatively simple tool works for individual as well as group discussions. It includes five steps for effective communication:

1. Goal statement

2. Conclusion

3. Key concepts and benefits

4. The ask – request commitment to action

5. Next steps

Preparation is key. Use this tool to gather your thoughts before your meeting. Be thoughtful and deliberate as you work on your message. Develop a roadmap to guide your conversation.

1. Start with the goal in mind – Create a clear goal statement for the meeting. Focus on results. Clearly identify what you want the participants to take away as a result of the discussion.

2. Identify the conclusion that you want listeners to reach at the end of the meeting – What key insight should they take away from the discussion.

3. Describe "why" the participant should listen and take action. Clearly articulate why this is important for them. Consider the specifics of what needs to be shared and consider how your team may respond. Think about the message from the participant's vantage point. Create the Pathway for the discussion. Identify the three to five key concepts that need to be addressed and the benefits that will be achieved from addressing them. The

ADKAR tool shared in the previous chapter provides guidance to help develop your message.

4. Prepare for any questions that your audience may have and ask for commitment.

5. Create an action-oriented close – Explain what will happen next.

This tool is intended to be your roadmap, not as a handout for your team. It will help you stay on point during conversations that can be challenging. Before your meeting take time to get yourself in the right mindset. Do some deep breathing to slow your heart rate and reduce your anxiety. At the start of your meeting, share what you want to achieve and explain why you asked for their time. Make sure to avoid irrelevant points, stay present in the moment and do not become defensive. Give brief answers as you respond to questions. Let the meeting participants do most of the talking. Stay curious about how participants are feeling. Listen for content, emotion and underlying meanings. Clarify what you are hearing so they know they have been heard. Stay resolute and ask participants to take the action requested. Inquire as to what they need to accomplish the goal. Stay positive and avoid making judgments. Focus on the behaviors and desired results. Agree on the next steps. Thank them for their attention, candid feedback and commitment as you move ahead.

Another key point to remember is that communication is not just about what you say. Your nonverbal messaging will have a significant impact to your believability. Nearly 90% of communication is not in the words you say but in your tone of voice, your posture and your eye movement. Pay attention to this as you deliver your message and you listen to what your audience has to say. How you deliver and how respond to what you hear is a reflection of your leadership and will determine how people take in what you say. Stay aware of what you are feeling. **Does your nonverbal language match your verbal content?** You are constantly communicating. Your communication can foster trust with deliberate attention. Clarify your values and set the example. Aligning your team requires that you model your own expectations as you build the case for change. The awareness and self-discipline discussed as part of the preparation phase is essential as you lead through the waves you will create.

Foster a Collaborative Environment

Healthcare is a team sport. It takes a great deal of cooperation, coordination and collaboration to deliver the care that patients require. Through the discussion about a "First Team," you learned about the importance of supporting versus competing with your peers and colleagues. Investing in the success of others allows you to be successful yourself. The same is true for your team. Be a leader that makes all team members feel valuable by ensuring that all points are heard and each individual takes responsibility for helping others to be successful. Collaboration fosters greater accountability, which grows trust and leads to team cohesion. Collaboration also encourages knowledge sharing between individuals and departments. This promotes innovation. This team collaboration can also surface potential issues so they can be proactively resolved. Be resolute and lead with the expectation that collaboration is nonnegotiable.

A baseline of trust is foundational to collaboration. Patrick Lencioni states that, "Trust is the confidence among team members that their peers' intentions are good, that there is no reason to be protective or careful around the group. In essence, teammates must get comfortable being vulnerable with one another." As the leader you are responsible for creating an environment where trust can grow. One of my own mantras is, "Assume positive intent." I truly believe that people, in general, are good and do not wish harm on others. People's intentions are far more often good than not. Although we may not always know the intention of others if we assume positive intent, we build trust more readily. Doing so we also avoid blaming others. We ourselves are more likely to accept mistakes and model that behavior in others. An overarching willingness to own weaknesses and accept mistakes promotes trust among team members. Role model your own vulnerability and willingness to accept the learning that comes from mistakes. When you openly share learning that comes from your own mistakes you encourage others to do the same. It may be overwhelming to imagine that every individual on your team would be comfortable sharing their weaknesses and mistakes. Lead by example toward this aspiration. Encourage it in your formal and informal leaders first. Grow the expectation and culture from there.

"Teamwork is the most statistically significant predictor of quality as perceived by patients, families and doctors." – E. C. Murphy, Relationship-Based Care

Donna Wright, the author of the teamwork chapter in *Relationship-Based Care, A Model for Transforming Practice*, shares the one consistent element to healthy productive teams is relationship management. This requires helping team members interact with one another in a healthy and productive way. Although it would be nice to assume that highly trained professionals just know how to interact with one another, many times they do not. Each individual brings their collective being to the team and many stories, judgements and assumptions are created. Helping the team grow as a "team" must be a part of your leadership vision. In *Relationship Based Care*, the authors share a tool created by Marie Manthey, called "Commitment to My Co-worker for Health Care Teams." It contains nine commitments that address behaviors to build trust, mutual respect, and support open, honest communication. This commitment concept is another tool for you. You can use the tool shared in *Relationship-Based Care* or have your team create their own tool. Regardless, it is about your team committing to a standard set of behaviors that promotes commitment to each other for the patient. Leading your team to collaboration by creating an environment with a guiding principle of "the good of the whole" will support the success of any and all goals established.

"Teamwork is the secret that makes common people achieve uncommon results." – Ifeanyi Enoch Onuoha, author, entrepreneur

Empower Your Team

According to Meriam Webster, empower means "to give official authority or legal power to; to enable; to promote the self-actualization or influence of." The combination of these three definitions is what empowering your looks like – to give them the authority to make decisions when possible, enable the ownership of their work, to promote and support their development to impact decisions and to enhance their autonomy. The term "empowerment" has been in nursing literature for as long as I can remember. I previously spoke about the abundant research that exists to support empowerment and its positive impact on nurses' practice environment. Since the early 80s, Tim Porter O'Grady and many other nursing pioneers have shared their wisdom regarding the importance of empowering nurses to enable decision-making over their own practice. Based on my personal experience, nurses who feel more empowered have a higher job satisfaction, are more curious and interested in improvement, are more committed to their work and are less likely to quit. Taking action to empower your team will create a positive environment for them to flourish.

One of my favorite examples of empowerment is illustrated in *Turn the Ship Around: A True story of Turning Followers into Leaders* by L. David Marquet, a retired U.S. Navy Captain. Marquet commandeered the nuclear-powered USS Santa Fe submarine from 1999 to 2001. He shares his learning as he tells the story of taking the worst submarine in the fleet to the best. When first assigned the command, Marquet found himself in foreign territory, not knowing the intricate workings of this new submarine. Additionally, the crew was inattentive and demoralized. In fact, the Santa Fe was used as an example of "what not to be." Marquet decided that he needed to fundamentally change how he led and interacted with the crew in order to create the turnaround his superiors were expecting. He needed his crew to work differently. He implemented what he calls a "leader-leader" model verses the typical "leader-follower" model. According to Marquet, "The leader-leader structure is fundamentally different from the leader-follower structure. At its core is the belief that we can all be leaders and, in fact, it's best when we all are leaders. Leadership is not some mystical quality that some possess and others do not. As humans, we all have what it takes, and we all need to use our leadership." He also suggests that, "if there's one thing people like more than following it is being followed." Rather than everyone waiting on his orders, he allowed (and expected) his crew the space to think about what they were doing and then share their intent. This created an ownership mentality among the crew. He turned the crew from "worst to best" by disrupting the standard practices and expecting leadership at all levels in every position.

Throughout the book Marquet shares tactics he used as he implemented the leader-leader model. According to Marquet, in order to realize every individual thinking like a leader, three key components are required: control, competence and clarity. When all three components exist, they reinforce one another and create a positive spiral.

- *Control* – Decentralized control refers to the freedom and authority to make decisions about your own work. The goal is to delegate decision-making control as far as possible into the organization.

  LEADER ACTION – Consider reworking processes, change mindsets by expecting new behavior, think aloud with your team, use regular check-ins to align and educate team members. Hold your team accountable for thinking, not just following. Encourage your team to think at the next level. Have your team bring you solutions, not just problems. Be willing to hear feedback.

- *Competence* – For decentralized control to work, individuals must be technically competent to make the right decisions. If you give people responsibility without equipping them with the required knowledge and resources, chaos ensues.

LEADER ACTION – Develop your team and ensure they have the ability to accept more responsibility. When you're asked for approval, flip it around and ask "what do you think I'm considering?" Understand that mistakes are helpful in learning what proper procedures should be implemented. Expect deliberate action and continuous learning.

- *Clarity* – For people at all levels to make effective decisions, they must be fully aligned with the organization's purpose, and thoroughly understand the organization's goals and decision-making criteria.

LEADER ACTION – Tie daily activities to broad goals and objectives. Help your team see how they are contributing and making a difference. Provide guidelines for decision making. Clearly communicate values and expectations. Model the way.

The story of the USS Santa Fe is an extraordinary example of empowerment. There are powerful lessons to consider for your own leadership in your own department. Strive to evolve to a "leader-leader" model. Create an ownership mentality among your team. Empower your team by giving them more responsibility, which will make them more productive. Resist the urge to provide solutions when challenges come up. Coach and support them to find solutions themselves. When they come to you seeking solutions:

- If urgent – provide a solution, and then have your team critique it.

- If it can wait a moment – ask the team for their input, then act.

- If it can wait a while – facilitate team discussion and have them propose solutions (it's okay if they don't all agree)

Engage them in leading the department, ask them:

- What's keeping you from doing your job better?

- What are our biggest challenges?

- What are your biggest frustrations about how our business is currently being run?

- What solutions do you have?

- What is the best thing I can do for you?

"People want guidance, not rhetoric; they need to know what the plan of action is and how it will be implemented. They want to be given responsibility to help solve the problem and the authority to act on it." – Howard Schultz, businessman, Starbucks CEO

Does your team simply follow rules because "they've been told to do it?" How do you encourage team members to think proactively? How do you share your leadership decision making process with your team? Do your people know how to help make leadership decisions? If your organization has a shared governance model, leverage it. If it does not, create a practice council to assist you when decisions can be delegated. Challenge yourself to delegate all that you can. As the proverb goes "Give a man a fish and he will eat for a day. Teach a man how to fish and you feed him for a lifetime." Teach your team how to fish and then expect them to fish. In other words, teach them how to own their issues and problems – to own the business.

Teach them how to collaboratively identify solutions and then teach them to own those solutions. Get their input, opinions, commitment to the decision and insist on accountability to those commitments. Growing a culture that supports empowerment is an ongoing process. Growing a culture that supports empowerment requires ongoing deliberate care and feeding. Build habits from the start that support the empowerment of your team. Look for those opportunities to empower them. The payoff will be tremendous.

"One of the greatest things you can do to help others is not just to share and give what you have, but to help them discover what they have within themselves." – Rita Zahara, chef, entrepreneur

In Captain Marquet's story of the USS Santa Fe you learned of the importance of delegating authority or decentralizing control. Although, essential to empower your team, appropriately delegating authority can be challenging. The decision to delegate is situational. It is dependent on the decision, the timing and the ability of the individuals to make a sound decision. To help you determine decisions that can or should be delegated use the "Level of Authority Decision Making Framework." This tool shared below creates a common language for everyone and provides clarity regarding decision responsibility. A key to empowerment is providing employees the means for making important decisions and helping them follow through on the decision they make. When as the leader, you assign a level of authority to a decision, you clearly articulate who owns the decision-making authority. You also are clearly communicating who owns ensuring follow-through and the consequences of the decisions made.

Figure: Level of Authority Decision Making Framework

Level of Authority Decision Making Framework
"As the leader I am giving you Level _ Authority"
meaning...
- **Level 1** – I decide
- **Level 2** – I decide with your input
- **Level 3** – We decide together, I maintain authority
- **Level 4** – You decide with my input
- **Level 5** – You decide

To explain a bit further:

- *Level 1*: "I decide" (the leader decides) – These decisions typically require immediate action and performance needs to be compliant without hesitation. The leader is in the best position because of clarity and knowledge to make the decision. Level 1 decision-making should be used sparingly if you want to create an empowered culture where everyone is contributing at their highest level. Level 1 authority is typically exerted during disastrous situations or following serious safety events until the right mitigating processes can be put into place.

  LEADER ACTION – Make decision, communicate decision importance, provide strong direction, support team through change and ensure follow-through.

- *Level 2*: "I decide with your input" (the leader decides with input) – These decisions are those that require input in order to be made, whether that is covering blind spots or learning more about the depth of the situation. In addition, this level is used when making the decision without key insights of specific people. In other words, when the cost of failure is high, the leader must decide. The leader seeks input but ultimately has the right to make the decision independently.

LEADER ACTION – Get input from key individuals, make decision, communicate decision and importance, leverage those who gave input, provide strong direction, support team through change and ensure follow-through.

- *Level 3*: "We decide together, I maintain authority" (the leader builds consensus with input from the group, and the leader has final decision) – At this level, the leader calls on the group or subgroup to gather feedback and come to some resolution. This is especially useful when a decision will have a profound impact on the group, and the team needs to debate, discern and decide together. This approach can take time since reaching a consensus means that "we all agree and we can all live with the decision." If consensus cannot be reached, the leader weighs all recommendations and decides.

  LEADER ACTION – Gather feedback, facilitate discussions, work through disagreements, build consensus if possible, make the decision, work with team to communicate decision and importance, leverage those who gave input, provide coaching and direction, support team through change and ensure follow-through.

- *Level 4*: You decide with my input (the group decides with input from the leader) – These decisions are those within the scope of the group, requiring a consensus from the group. The leader provides input in the form of coaching or sharing consequences. The authority and responsibility shift from the leader, who reviews the decision but does not change it. The leader provides support in execution and may use the decision as an opportunity for development. This level is useful when the leader sets some boundaries around the decision and gives authority within those boundaries. I have often, successfully used this level, particularly when I gave teams "non-negotiables" to be followed, and then given them free reign. It is best to provide a timeline for when a decision needs to be made in order to prevent ongoing debate.

LEADER ACTION – Facilitate discussions, provide guidance, share wisdom and perspective, work through disagreements, support team decision, work with team to communicate decision importance and respond to feedback, provide coaching, facilitate peer-to-peer coaching and share ownership to ensure follow-through.

- *Level 5*: You decide (the group decides) – These decisions are at the full discretion of the group; the leader fully delegates the decision to a group and becomes one of many. The group discusses, discerns and decides on behalf of the organization. The leader supports the decision made.

LEADER ACTION – Encourage discussions, share wisdom and perspective if asked, support team's decision, help team communicate decision and importance, direct feedback to the team and coach individuals to facilitate peer-to-peer responsibility to ensure follow-through.

The key here is transparency so everyone is on the same page about how the decision will be made, who is making the decision, why the decision is being made in a particular way, and who owns deployment of the decision. To be most effective, educate you team. Create a common language about decision authority. Share what level you are using and why. Consider the appropriate level of authority for you and your team to avoid confusion. The transparency you will achieve builds clarity. Delegating authority promotes their development as professionals. Delegate authority when you can. Ask yourself:

- "Who maintains authority for making the final decision?" If you want to maintain "veto" power – that is not Level 4 or 5. It is Level 1, 2, or 3.

- "How much input will I allow?" If you are only getting input from a few stakeholders, this is likely Level 2 (maybe even Level 1).

- "Is this an emergency that requires immediate action?" If yes, then this is a Level 1 decision and as the leader, you need to make it. If no, seek the appropriate level.

- "Is this something that I can support regardless of the decision?" If yes, this is a Level 5 decision. Give it to your team to decide and wholeheartedly support their decision

Most likely there will be few Level 1 or Level 5 decisions at you can delegate. Most will fall into Levels 2, 3 & 4. Strong leaders become savvy using all levels and own decision authority according to each level. Keep in mind that these levels of authority apply at all levels within the organization. Your boss and your boss's boss also delegate authority for decisions. Having clarity about the level of decision authority being delegated to you from your boss supports your own empowered leadership. You demonstrate empowerment by accepting full responsibility for what is yours to own.

Empowerment is essential to help your team grow. It is an important aspect of being a servant leader and is part of the five leadership practices and ten leadership commitments identified in *The Leadership Challenge*. Growing a culture of empowerment is ongoing and will require constant deliberate leadership to achieve. Your *READI* leadership will enable empowerment to blossom.

"Leadership is communicating to people their worth and potential so clearly that they are inspired to see it in themselves." – L. David Marquet, retired U.S. Naval captain

Manage Your Team's Talent

I hesitated to use the term "manage" in reference to your team's talent. However, according to Webster, to manage means to "handle or direct with a degree of skill such as to exercise executive, administrative, and supervisory direction." In your role as Nurse Manager, you will be required to exercise executive, administrative, and supervisory direction of the people who make up your team – to manage the talent you have been given responsibility. You are responsible to ensure that you have the right people, with the right skills, in the right numbers, doing the right things at the right time. You are responsible for ensuring that your team is performing to the established standards. From staffing and scheduling to hiring and discipline, there are numerous processes to assist. My wish for you is that you accomplish this through your *READI* leadership, rather than relying on a series of human resource policies as authority.

In his book, *Good to Great*, Jim Collins illustrates managing a team's performance using a bus analogy, "First get the right people on the bus, the wrong people off the bus, and the right people in the right seats, and then they can figure out where to drive it." Although, as a manager, you may not be determining where precisely the bus is going, but you are responsible for ensuring that your team members are both on the bus and in the right seats. You also need to ensure that the right number of seats are filled (we will discuss this further later). During the "discovery" phase, you assessed your team. You evaluated and will continue to evaluate their capability and performance collectively as a team and as individual contributors. You need to determine if they are meeting your expectations and the expectations of the organization. **Are they on the bus? Are they in the right seat on the bus?** Realistically, it would be hard to imagine an unequivocally "yes" response to both of these questions for everyone on your team. It is important to acknowledge the positives as well as the areas of concern. **What is driving the positive behavior? Is it team support or individual motivation? Are concerns stemming from team culture or individual capability? Is it skill or motivation? Is it lack of direction or a lack of clear expectations?**

You must determine if the team structure supports the work, and if each individual contributes to accomplishing the work. Both are important to managing performance and achieving the desired results. Structure alone will not resolve issues and individuals will not be successful in the wrong structure. For any performance issues identified, determine the root cause. It may be an individual, structure or culture problem. **Is the team organized and deployed to meet the department's objectives? Are decisions being made at the right place? Do you have the right structure and individuals in place? What support does your team need? Do these needs**

require a different structure? Take action as you discover your answers.

When assessing your team, be cautious about your assumptions. Rule out other causes before declaring you have the wrong people. Flaws you observe may simply be the result of team members needing healthy leadership. Before making the decision that you have the wrong people, do the work you need to do. Establish the expectations for performance and create the right structure to support meeting those expectations. With the right support framework, leverage the talent you have and manage individual performances for success. Performance management is an ongoing process. It requires ongoing feedback that reinforces desired behavior, feedback for improvement and feedback that redirects. As a general rule, people want to be part of an "A" team. Reinforce "A" team behaviors, give feedback to improve "B" behaviors and redirect "C" behaviors. If you fail to address B and C behaviors, you will not keep the A players that you want to keep. Berry Belcher, a serial entrepreneur in the digital marketing space, famously said, "Nothing will kill a great employee faster than watching you tolerate a bad one." Be resolute – do not ignore what should not be ignored. Take action to address what needs to be addressed. Ensure that you have the right people on the bus. Ensure that people are in the right seat on the bus. You may need to move individuals from one seat to another, and when necessary, invite the wrong people to get off the bus.

"Performance should be an expectation of employment and it is the leaders' job to create an environment where maximum performance is possible." –
Rob Burn, business consultant & performance coach

Addressing performance takes courage, deliberate action and resolve. The people you are responsible for are the reason your job exists. Lean into this responsibility. Be bold but kind. Take action early. At this point in your transition, in your first three months, ensure that you have the right structure and focus on the performance of key individuals in formal or informal leadership roles in your department. I will discuss this subject more later on in this book.

For now, make sure you have the right structure in place to support you and that you have the right people in roles that are extensions of you. Roles such as a charge nurse, for example, are making decisions when you are not there. Make sure the right talent is leveraged in these areas first. Individuals holding leadership roles need to demonstrate the leadership you expect. These individuals can help you influence the culture in the direction you want.

Build a Coalition

Communicating your vision and expectations, fostering team collaboration, empowering your team and managing your team's talent will support the creation of a solid foundation for your desired outcomes. You cannot achieve these results alone. You need a coalition of supporters to take action. Build community among your team and stakeholders. "Enable them to act" and "encourage their hearts," as discussed in *The Leadership Challenge*.

You are more likely to create followership through challenging times if your team believes that they have your support. As a leader, and in particular as a new leader, you will search for opportunities to change the status quo. You will look for innovative ways to improve the organization. You will make waves. Waves can be scary. Waves may threaten or overwhelm your team. Demonstrate that you have their backs, and coach, guide and support them as they experience challenges. Help them remove barriers. Ensure they know that you will support them as they grow to meet your expectations. Take action on their ideas. Strive to create an atmosphere of trust and human dignity, that strengthens others. Make them feel capable and powerful.

"The task of leadership is not to put passion into people, but to inspire and elicit it – for the passion is there already." – Ty Howard, speaker, author, consultant

Accomplishing extraordinary things is hard work. Encourage your team by celebrating even the small accomplishments. You need to accept occasional disappointments as opportunities to learn because innovation and change involve making mistakes. Reinforce this with your team by creating the habit of routine meaningful celebration. A great rule of thumb here – if things go well, your team deserves all of the credit. If things do not go as planned, as the leader, it is your job to accept responsibility and help your team enjoy the learning that comes from it. Recognize the specific contributions that individuals make. Let them know just how they are making a difference. Make your team feel like heroes. Connect with their hearts. When they feel appreciated, they will come together as a community united in purpose and achieve even more.

Execute

"The only impossible journey is the one you never begin." – Tony Robbins, motivational speaker & life coach

As you approach the end of your first 90 days, you are diving into your action plan by implementing the tactics established. Much of what has been discussed up to this point will support you in executing your plan. Taking action will result in successes and setbacks. You will have exciting days and frustrating days. Stay motivated by your purpose and what you want to accomplish. Stay vigilant to your presence and how you are leading to accomplish the tasks at hand. Stay focused on people while you manage the processes. As you execute your plan, keep your resolve. You are empowered to act. Be authentic and deliberate with your support and recognition. Keep your inquiring, learning mindset. Leverage your resources while using the quality management system and the change leadership tools. In addition to the material already shared, I want to emphasize three additional points as you progress through your strategy. First, building a habit of humble inquiry demonstrates a commitment to deeper learning. It promotes psychological safety in conversation so you can learn what is really happening. Second, taking action to drive change requires a focus on results with a disciplined process to quickly learn and adjust. Third, leading others requires credibility. Maintaining credibility through change requires intentional focus.

Humbly Inquiry

The *I* in *READI* leadership stands for "inquisitive." I have encouraged you to be inquisitive, to keep an inquiring mindset, a spirit for learning and to remain curious. I have encouraged you to tell less, to ask and listen more. This is the basis of humble inquiry. Have you ever been told to only ask the question if you know the answer? That is NOT the intent of humble inquiry. According to Edgar Schien, former MIT professor and father of organizational psychology, humble inquiry is "the skill and the art of drawing someone out, of asking questions to which you do not already know the answer, of building a relationship based on curiosity and interest in the other person." In his book, *Humble Inquiry,* Schein suggests that the act of asking is strength. It provides an atmosphere of caring, curiosity and collaboration. It is a reliable way of gathering data to prevent troublesome, knee-jerk reactions that can result from assumptions and judgments based on incomplete or incorrect data. This book is another "must have" for your library.

Consider this example: You get a call from the risk manager, and you need to investigate a safety event that occurred in your department. Based on the report, it appears that a team member did not follow the procedure. You need to understand what happened – why the task was completed in a way that appears problematic. You may assume that the associate intentionally cut corners or did not know the correct procedure. One approach of dealing with this is to ask your team member for an explanation and tell them the "right" way to do it. In this scenario, the subordinate is immediately put on the defensive, and you risk compromising trust and respect. Humble inquiry takes another approach: Assuming positive intent, imagine saying, "I would like to talk with you about the incident. It would help me to understand what happened. Would you walk me through the situation?" Listen attentively as the question is answered. Based on the response, you can ask additional, respectful (not leading) questions to get a complete understanding of why the individual took the steps they did. These questions will establish collaboration and get you to the root of the concern. You demonstrate that you care, while avoiding placing blame. From here you can now establish a commitment. The initial approach may lead to a quicker resolution, but it will not uncover the core issue and will likely create bigger problems in the future.

*"People do what they do because it made sense to them
at the time that they did it."* - Unknown

Building the habit to humbly inquire will take practice. Learning to inquire first takes deliberate thought. It requires authenticity. When I first learned about the importance of humble inquiry as a critical part of servant leadership, I found myself awkwardly asking questions, battling the thoughts in my head and not listening to what someone really said to me. I slowly learned to become more vulnerable and got comfortable with not knowing the right answer. I learned to embrace the interdependence of the relationship with others. I leveraged my authenticity and shared that I was building a new skill. I told my team that I needed their help as I practiced. I felt awkward. They were more than happy to allow me to stumble as I practiced. Through practice, I became better at engaging them in a healthier way. I realized that as the leader, helping someone develop problem-solving skills meant that I needed to create the space for them to do so. Learning humble inquiry enabled me to ask respectful questions that proved my dedication to them. It was a way of demonstrating I cared about their knowledge, experiences and thoughts. In group settings the practice of humble inquiry encourages everyone's participation. It is a way of hearing everyone's contribution before moving to solutions.

Schien describes humble inquiry as an art. It takes intention, focus and practice. What we ask, how we ask, when and where we ask are all important aspects of humble inquiry. Our verbal and nonverbal language matters as we establish rapport. It matters as we create a culture of safety and collaboration. Dave Galloway, founder and principal of Continuous MILE Consulting, blogs about leadership, continuous improvement, safety and innovation. In an article titled, "Control or Caring? What is Your Motive for a Safety Conversation," he states, "If you want compliance, then manage through control, criticism, and correction. If you seek commitment, then lead through caring, coaching, and collaboration." Humble inquiry is a mechanism to lead through caring, coaching and collaboration. Consider the fall example shared previously. If you were seeking control, the associate would likely feel criticized, and may briefly answer your questions. But they won't likely share what they were thinking or why they made a particular decision. Not having this information would compromise your ability to fully understand the situation and potential risk to other patients if unresolved. You are much more likely to discover the real issue (process barriers, broad knowledge deficits, lack of supplies/resources) by using a more humble approach. If your desire is to lead in a manner that will build commitment to improve care delivery, humble inquiry is an essential skill. Galloway suggests, "If the reason you have any conversation is because you care, the approach will naturally be to coach and seek commitment through collaboration." Pay attention to your "why" as you engage in any conversation. Make your "why" about caring – caring to learn, caring to build relationships, caring to support the others' development, and caring to create a safe environment for your team and their colleagues to practice. Any or all of these may be the perfect reasons "why."

In his book, Schien goes into great detail about the many benefits and the science behind why humble inquiry works. He suggests (and based on my own experience seeing the result, I wholeheartedly agree) it is essential to exceptional leadership. And it is critical to develop your *READI* leadership. As you are growing your brand and developing your leadership build the habit as you start:

- Ask respectful questions – Use open-ended questions. This allows for open-ended answers, promotes thinking and deeper sharing of thoughts. You are signaling that you need their help. The person being questioned is encouraged to thoughtfully participate in dialogue.

- Refrain from "yes or no," "would you agree," or "have you thought of" questions – These questions are leading questions indicating you are seeking agreement or that you are leading someone to an answer you already know. Ask 'what' questions.

- Actively and attentively listen – Assume that you have something to discover from the answer (you do). Focus on the true meaning of what is being said. Listen for content, emotion and underlying meaning, not just the words being used. Focus on what the speaker is sharing. Clarify what you hear.

- Focus – Pay attention to the person you are questioning. Remember, you are coming from a place of caring. Concentrate on the person, not the problem. Being attentive can help you see the emotion being shared, and you can gain deeper insight to the meaning. Your peeked curiosity will lead you to discover more.

Use your authenticity. Show you care about the person. Be deliberate in your word choice and your posture. Empower the other person. Inquire to discover what others are thinking. Invite alternative perspectives and listen for dissent. Engage in the dialogue that comes with asking when you do not know the answer. Celebrate the learning that you receive. Let your light shine in order to help the light grow in others.

"Listening is being able to be changed by the other person." – Alan Alda, actor, director, & screenwriter

Focus on Results

Keep your eye on the prize. Stay resolute to your goal and flexible with your plan. As you put the tactics from your plan into place, you will see that some work and some do not. This requires deliberate monitoring of both process and results. Use both leading and the lagging indicators to monitor progress and stay on track. In most instances, the lagging indicators are the outcomes that you are trying to improve. Lagging indicators are often reported as events or rates. Some examples of lagging indicators include the number of serious safety events, patient satisfaction data, infection rates, turnover or a budget variance. A leading indicator is a predictive measurement. It is a data point, often a process measure, that points to a future event. An example of a leading indicator may be the compliance with identified processes to reduce urinary tract infections or the number of times a patient needs to use their call light. Both are important as you lead to improve care.

Let me explain further using an example. If your desire is to prevent patient falls, your goal is zero falls. Your lagging indicator is the number of falls that occur. As you study why falls occur, you and your team will deploy new processes. Your leading indicators should coincide with the intervention(s) deployed to reduce falls. It may be compliance with assessing risk, or compliance staying with patients when assisted to the bathroom. Your leading indicator is predictive, while the lagging indicator evaluates past events. Without the leading indicator you are driving for results looking through the rear-view mirror. Imagine driving your car and trying to get to your destination while only looking at the rear-view mirror. You may (although unlikely) end up where you want to go, but imagine the frustrations that you would feel and the destruction you would cause. Similarly, you cannot improve care delivery processes if you focus your monitoring and learning only on the lagging indicators. If you only focus on the occurrence of a fall, you will miss so much of what can be learned. You miss potential early signs that may lead to patients falling. You're too late – the event you are trying to prevent has already happened. You want to study a fall should it occur, but to determine what leading indicator may have been missed and what may need to change. When you study leading indicators, you are more likely to identify risks and intervene proactively. The PDSA rapid cycle change method can be very effective here. The PDSA cycle directs you and your team to create and understand the leading indicators to be tracked. Leading indicators are the key performance indicators (KPIs) to monitor. They are intended to "lead"' you to successfully meet your objective. Coupled with humble inquiry, PDSA will support an environment of learning, collaboration, empowerment and continuous improvement. I want to dive a bit deeper into PDSA, KPIs and visual management to help you and your team focus on results.

To review, PDSA forces a vigilant monitoring of a process so you can understand the root cause and apply the right remedy. It serves as a great tool to engage your team, provide an avenue to celebrate success and identify the impact of changes. To use the PDSA cycle, start with what you are trying to accomplish (your aim). This may be your SMART goal. Determine how the change leads to improvement. Work with your team to:

- Plan – Establish a process change. Plan the test or observation. State the objective of the test. Make a prediction(s) regarding what will happen and why. Integrate what you have learned from the six sources of influence into your plan. Determine the KPI(s) to be measured. Develop a plan to test the change (Who? What? When? Where?) Create a plan to collect the data. Create a plan to make the data visual.

- Do – Try it on a small scale. Test your planned intervention. Document observations and problems. Ask yourself: did you get what you expected? Gather data. Monitor your KPI.

- Study – Analyze the data and study the results. Compare the data to your predictions. Summarize findings and reflect on what was learned. Determine if the intervention should be adopted, adapted or abandoned. Apply the analysis to the next step.

- Act – Refine the change based on results from test. Determine what modifications should be made. Prepare a plan for the next test.

KPIs are often a process measure or a measure of compliance completing a task that is intended to drive outcomes (an example of a leading indicator). Once you identify the right processes, consistently meeting results relies on consistent process execution. You and your team are more likely to achieve success with a relentless adherence to processes. Consistency is key. This is easier said than done. There are a variety of factors that may interrupt this consistency. The process of monitoring process KPIs provides the ability to identify these factors. Studying "why" when the KPI fails to meet standards and develop corrective measures will help to minimize or eliminate the factors that prevent successful adherence to the process – and ultimately the outcome you are trying to achieve. With understanding comes further problem solving. The more often KPI data is collected, the more effectively the outcome can be managed. I suggest daily whenever possible. Identify a process that data can be collected easily, even if it is self-reported, so that it can be reviewed frequently. Once collected, determine if it meets the standard expected. Work with your team to take the appropriate action. Leading your team to facilitate the development, collection, monitoring and evaluating of KPIs will promote their ownership and their empowerment.

"Always remember, your focus determines your reality." – George Lucas, director, producer, & screenwriter

Use visual management. Visual management is a way to visually communicate results that does not require training. You can use visual management to illustrate process compliance as well as to illustrate or guide the completion of the process itself. First, make the KPI visual by using graphs or charts to show results, progress and trends. Visuals are an impactful way of showing results (pictures are worth a thousand words). Your team can see the work without the need for explanation. This promotes the movement to problem solving more quickly. When results are hidden in stacks of documents, it is easy to ignore the information or hide the problem. Secondly, using visual management to guide the process itself supports busy care givers in the midst of providing care. We have used visual management in our nursing practice for decades. We have used special armbands in the past to alert team members about resuscitation status or fall risk. We have used visual management to prevent using a limb for venipuncture We have used visual management in our signage above patient beds. We have used visual management to label supply cabinets. Engage your team and challenge them to think creatively about how to leverage visual management successfully.

Asking humble questions and listening to the thoughts of others, leveraging PDSA to quickly learn and make improvements, tracking the right KPIs that will lead to the outcomes desired and using visual management will help you execute your plan more effectively. Bring these tools all together in a deliberate and routine way. Establish a process for deliberate, methodical review. Set a time every day to discuss the KPIs with your team. Review the results and do some quick investigating and problem solving. Assign follow-ups and help your team complete the assigned tasks. Escalate what needs to be escalated. Be cautious to *not* take responsibility for all follow-ups. Empower your team to take ownership. Build the habit to have daily huddles. Expect attendance by everyone. Expect participation and facilitate the KPI review process. If a defect occurs, study it. Discuss it briefly and determine how the root cause will be identified. Based on the findings, work with your team to determine the next steps to be taken.

There are many tools to help support you and your team, such as fishbone diagraming, process mapping, flow-charting and cause-and-effect analysis. Each provides a disciplined approach to problem resolution. I will not go into detail about all of them, it is important you are aware these tools exist to help you investigate problems, identify contributing factors and determine the right solutions. You can quickly learn how to use them with a bit of internet surfacing. Whatever process improvement tools are used, take a disciplined review of the facts, study trends and only then identify and test the solution. We can easily get trapped in what seems like an "easy" or "quick" solution, only to find out that it does not solve the real problem. Engage your team in each step of the process. Facilitate discussions and help them work through the steps. Work with them to determine the actions to take. Help them own the monitoring process. Role model how to challenge the process. Enable them to take action when the desired outcome is not achieved. Help them discover what can be learned from setbacks.

"Every strike brings me closer to the next home run." – George Herman "Babe" Ruth, professional baseball player

Celebrate every discovery. Thomas Edison said, after many attempts to create the light bulb, "I haven't failed, I've just found 10,000 ways that won't work." As you search for innovative ways to improve care delivery, you and your team will be taking risks. You will discover things that do not work. As the leader, you must accept the disappointments and learn from each opportunity. Do not place blame. Do not become disheartened. Share the impact and celebrate the steps taken. An unknown wise individual once said, "The best leaders look in the mirror when things are not going well and look through a window when things are going well." As the leader, you must take responsibility when things do not go as planned and help your team learn from the discoveries. If things work, make it all about the team. Recognize them for their great efforts and celebrate them. Make them the heroes. Share your wins with your boss. It will give fuel to your fire and serve as a genuine opportunity for your boss to recognize your team.

Lead with Credibility

Credibility is the foundation of leadership, but can be easily damaged with lack of intention.

Credibility is built in all that you say and do. As you prepare to execute your plan, I encourage you to deliberately pay attention to growing your credibility. As the manager of your department, you are the *one* everyone on your team is watching. You are constantly on stage and your team is watching the production. This is the reality of the position you hold. You may have 10 or 110 staff members, regardless, your attention is divided among all of them. Theirs is on you. They are watching you, determining if they will follow you. Barbara Kellerman, professor of public leadership at Harvard, suggests that, "Followers are more important to leaders than leaders are to followers." Your success relies on your team following you. As you start your new role, there is only one chance to make a first impression. You started growing your credibility bank immediately when you started. During times of turmoil, stress or change you risk making credibility withdrawals if you fail to act with deliberate intention. As you work with your team to implement change, growing and maintaining your credibility is vital to make certain that your team is coming with you to your destination.

James Kouzes and Barry Posner assert that we follow the people we believe to be credible – competent, honest, forward thinking and inspirational. They submit the first law for leaders is, "People will not believe the message if they do not believe in the messenger." Their second law for leaders is "Do what you say you will do." Gaining followership does not come with position and authority. It comes with belief. According to Merriam Webster, credibility is defined as the "quality or power of inspiring belief." **Why should anyone believe you?** Consistency in behavior, words, actions and modeling what you expect supports that belief. **Are you demonstrating what you expect from others? Do you instill belief in your words and actions?** It is likely that your organization has established principles concerning the way people (constituents, peers, colleagues and customers) should be treated and how goals should be pursued. As the department leader, you create the example for your team. You set the model for others to follow. Be authentic and deliberately consistent – consistency in organizational standards, your behavior, what you say, how you demonstrate your values, how you treat your colleagues, how you demonstrate collaboration across departments, how you resolve conflict and how you treat individuals on your team. Consistency builds trust and credibility.

Credibility is a meaty subject, a subject way more deserving than a couple of paragraphs. Kouzes and Posner have written an entire book on the subject. Bottom line, if you are going to lead, you need followers. In order to have followers, you must have credibility. Your success relies on your team following you. Following is an act of trust and faith in the course of the leader. That faith can only be generated if leaders have credibility. Your *READI* leadership provides the foundation for your credibility.

"If you think you're leading but no one is following, then you're just taking a walk." – John C. Maxwell, pastor, author. coach & speaker

Your first 90 days is coming to a close and you are actively leading your team by taking the steps to accomplish the goals established. You have taken in a great deal of information through your onboarding. There is much that you want to accomplish. There is much to still discover, your learning is not over. As you transition into the next phase of your journey, take time to reflect. It is a great time to adjust your leadership based on what you now know. Reflection with focused adjustment will strengthen your *READI* leadership as you continue to grow your competencies and execute your strategy.

90 Days: Align & Execute

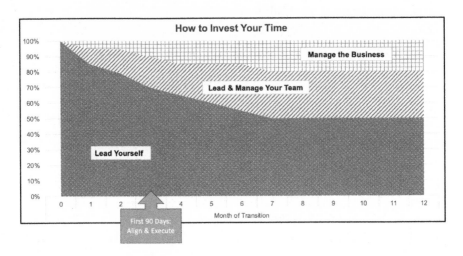

Actions to take:

✓ Manage your calendar

  – Further deploy your visibility plan

  – Continue to progress through your relationship heat map

  – Continue to check off the processes you are learning and doing independently

✓ Communicate your vision and expectations

✓ Establish effective team structures and team ground-rules for collaboration

✓ Address immediate performance issues

✓ Leverage organization structure for shared governance or create your own practice council

✓ Delegate authority to your team where and when possible

✓ Use a quality management system and tools for executing your plan

✓ Use change leadership tools to execute your plan

✓ Practice humbly inquiring and grow your "humble inquiry" skills

✓ Identify leading and lagging indicators that tie into readily available data points (KPIs) that can be monitored

✓ Start a daily KPI review huddle and utilize visual management tools to make your KPIs come to life

✓ Establish a process to identify and study defects

✓ Learn from any set-backs

✓ Share key learnings and accomplishments with your boss

✓ Celebrate any and all accomplishments

Tools shared:

✓ Five Steps to Effective Communication

✓ Commitment to My Co-Worker

✓ Level of Authority

Must have for your library:

✓ *Humble Inquiry* by Edgar Schein – it will change the way you lead and coach your team; it will foster deeper connections with your colleagues

Quick tip hints for success:

✓ Ask for help

✓ Always start by assuming the positive intent of others and reframe your thinking to create the possibility of others coming from a positive place

✓ Keep asking patients to share what they notice about care delivery (use humble inquiry to understand the deeper meaning of their experience and what is most important to them)

✓ Plan for the capital resources you may need. Capital investments must be planned. Determine if your team/department requires any capital investments. Ask your boss/mentor or finance team partners to define "capital" in your organization. Start planning for the requests that you will be making.

✓ It is *as* important to understand why your department runs favorable to budget, *as* it is to understand why your department may be unfavorable to budget. Both too many resources or too few resources result in challenges that need to be managed. Leverage your mentor relationship to help you complete an operating budget variance report. Complete it even if your department had favorable labor or expense variances.

CHAPTER SEVEN
6 Months: Reflect & Adjust

This phase of the journey requires introspection and vulnerability. You've shifted more time into leading your team and managing the business. Your leadership of self must remain a focus as well. Now is a good time to pause and reflect. Reflection helps to determine where adjustments need to be made in order to more effectively execute your strategy. You can compare this with the "evaluation" stage of the nursing process or the "check" phase of any performance improvement cycle. You have been on a journey to discover and learn in order to define your priorities. You created a plan and have taken steps to execute your plans. You have grown awareness of your leadership. You have established relationships that you want to foster and grow. You have supported your colleagues. You have encouraged and engaged with your team to improve care and grow their leadership. You have focused on what you want to achieve and how you lead to accomplish your aspirations. Be inquisitive and keep a learning mindset as you reflect on your past three months. Be deliberate about what you want to adjust. Stay resolute in your purpose and empowered to do what is right. Be authentic and genuine, Let your light shine and inspire the light in others. Your *READI* leadership will facilitate your look back to move forward.

"Life can only be understood backwards; but it must be lived forwards." - Søren Kierkegaard, – Danish philosopher, theologian, poet, author

Reflect On Your Leadership

Look back so you can move forward. It is likely that you have been burning the candle from both ends – working long hours, drinking from that fire hose with your head down, plowing through your to-do list. You have dedicated your time to ensuring that you meet the needs of your patients, team, medical staff, boss, and colleagues. It is essential to periodically pause and examine your leadership. In Michael Watkin's book, *The First 90 Days,* he suggests that your successes or failures stem from every small choice you make along the way. He goes on to say that these choices either create the momentum for success, or turn into vicious cycles that undermine your effectiveness. You cannot lead others if you are not effectively leading yourself. Leading yourself requires an honest look in the mirror. It requires self-awareness and self-discipline. **How are things going for you? How are the choices you have made serving you? How is your leadership gaining followers? How are the actions you have taken making an impact?** As you reflect, look for opportunities to celebrate Show gratitude for what has been accomplished.

The ANOL specifically calls out reflective practices as key competencies within the Nurse Manager competency framework developed. Regularly engaging in a reflective practice should be a part of your personal development journey. It is not a luxury but critical to optimizing the leader within you. The practice of self-reflection is important. All too often I see leaders so focused on the daily tasks and the daily issues needing to be solved they fail to see the bigger picture of their role. They fail to see the impact of their leadership on their team and the care provided. They are so committed to the department and their team they fail to focus on their own leadership which actually stalls their leadership effectiveness. Think about this reflection practice on two levels. First reflection completed during intentionally scheduled uninterrupted time dedicated to review the impact of your leadership. And second, self-reflection in the moment. The first requires making a reflection day a priority and forcing yourself to take a step back and review. The second is a skill to be developed a muscle to strengthen and an opportunity to grow emotional intelligence, credibility and confidence. Both will strengthen your *READI* leadership.

Early in my own leadership journey, I found myself in a vicious cycle. I was frustrated. I worked harder I and spent more time at work. I tried different tactics to address the department problems. It was the advice of a mentor that forced me to think differently about what I was doing. To be honest, I was initially offended at his advice. He told me that I needed to be more selfish with my time. Selfishness was offensive to me – I was a servant after all. This is a paradox that I will discuss further in the upcoming chapter. My mentor said that I needed to be "appropriately selfish." I needed to give myself permission to step back, step away and reflect so that I could be more strategic. My mentor helped me see that my team needed me to lead differently, and it was through my reflection practice that I was able to figure out how to do this. With work, I built new habits, and it made a huge difference for me as a leader.

Leaders who take the time to reflect on past events stand out. They are more likely to test assumptions, make connections and improve their leadership capacity. They are more effective. Be deliberate. Schedule time to reflect. Use this time to review your thoughts, decisions and emotions. This investment in your time will have a significant return for you. The completion of your first three months in the role, is a great time to reflect and determine the way forward. Through your transition journey, you have met with numerous people. You received a great deal of feedback. Give yourself some meaningful objective feedback. Prioritize a day away from your department where you can reflect and strategize. Take the day to be appropriately selfish and relax. Be thoughtful and thoroughly review your leadership. Be deliberate about your reflection and be inquisitive as you reflect. Do not make judgments about what you discover as you reflect. Focus on learning and enhancing awareness to adjust where you need to adjust (I will share a tool shortly to get specific on what to change). Identify the key learning points so your next three months can be even more effective.

Ask yourself the questions below. Be intellectually honest with yourself. Avoid the urge to cast shame and judgment about your answers.

- **How are things going?**

- **How do you feel so far?**

- **What has bothered you so far?**

- **What has gone well? – why?**

- **What has not gone well? – why not?**

- **How have you been showing up as a leader? Are people following you? How do you know?**

- **Are you gaining commitment to your vision and goals? How do you know?**

- **How can you use your authority to control less and influence more?**

- **What feedback have you received?**

- **Are you getting the results you want?**

- **What should be celebrated?**

- **Who should be recognized?**

- **Are the choices you made serving you well? Or do you find yourself in a cycle that is damaging your leadership?**

- **Are the actions you have taken making an impact? How do you know?**

- **How are you really? How is your energy and enthusiasm? What would others say if they answered for you?**

This practice of stepping back and looking objectively inward will help you discover meaning, form connections and create pathways to future learning. The deeper the reflection, the deeper the exploration will be, and the greater the learning. In his book, *Flying Without a Net,* Thomas DeLong explains how to draw from the vulnerability that comes from reflection. He submits that when we understand our anxiety triggers and the unproductive behaviors we turn to for relief, we can determine the new behaviors we should adopt. Delong's research identifies the root of high achiever's anxiety stems from a fear of being wrong, a lack of purpose and/or craving human connection. **Is this true for you?** According to his research, common destructive behaviors that high achievers commonly adopt to relieve their anxiety is busyness, comparing ourselves to others and blaming others for our frustrations. **Do these behaviors describe your behavior?**

"Always walk through life as if you have something new to learn and you will." – Vernon Howard, spiritual teacher, author, & philosopher

Ultimately, reflection should become a part of your daily routines. According to Nick Wignall, a clinical psychologist and therapist, "self-reflection becomes vastly more powerful when we can use it in real-time to make better decisions." Self-reflection, in the moment, is a skill to grow, and with deliberate practice, will become a habit. The most effective leaders have a greater sense of the world around them – they are more aware and insightful. How? They are deliberate about learning. They regularly work to widen their awareness in the moment, while paying attention to their blind spots. When you maintain a learning, self-aware mindset, you are not fixed on your own beliefs and answers, but are willing to see another perspective and grow insight. When you are open to understanding what drives your own behaviors, you can more effectively regulate your behavior, resulting in better decision-making. Start with an intentional review as you commute home at the end of the day. Review your decisions, actions and their impact. This reflective practice will help grow your awareness and effectiveness as a leader.

In an article titled, "The Elements of Self-Reflection," Wignall offers three independent but interconnected skills to achieve optimal self-reflection:

- *Maintain openness* – awareness of your "go-to" responses. **What are your default beliefs that influence your thinking? Where do they come from? Are they serving you well?** Openness means becoming aware of and free from inherited beliefs and stereotypes about you and the world, while learning to see things as they are versus what you think or thought they were.

ACTIONS TO TAKE – keep a decision journal and a log of the factors that influence your decisions, particularly those decisions that tend to be automatic; ask "why" until you have the accurate influencers recorded. When you become more aware of what is behind your decisions, you will be more likely to consider alternatives.

- *Observe* – pay attention to what you feel during high-stress times (chest tightness, nausea, shoulder or neck aches) because your body is telling you something; watch yourself as if you were watching a movie. **What do you see? What sensations do you feel?** Observation provides perspective.

ACTIONS TO TAKE – practice mindfulness meditation to develop the skills to deliberately shift your attention outward, versus the autonomic inward response controlled by your amygdala. Building the skills to shift your thinking outward will enable you to walk through high-stress situations more rationally.

- *Maintain objectivity* – separate your thoughts, feelings and behaviors from your sense of self – they are only a part of who you are. **What stories are you telling yourself? Do you have evidence (facts) that your story is correct? What else may be true?** Objectivity means understanding that you are more than the product of your thoughts, feelings and behaviors.

ACTIONS TO TAKE – Keep a thought diary and record the relationship between your thoughts, emotions and behaviors; identify your triggers and responses. This helps to reframe your thoughts to be more fact-based which will support healthier responses.

Becoming more deliberate in your reflection practice will strengthen your emotional intelligence. By looking inward, beyond what happened, you will begin to experience deeper awareness and enhance your credibility. You will gain clarity on your core values, enabling you to act with a higher degree of integrity and make better decisions. You will become more confident, which will give you the strength and courage to lead.

Before I move on, I want to discuss a few additional topics to contemplate during your reflection: How you are leading through your relationships, how you are leading to develop your team and how you are leading yourself. Each topic is an important aspect for your ongoing success and deliberate focus in your leadership journey.

Leading Through Your Relationships

Early in your onboarding I discussed the importance of people. I stressed the need for you to make a list of all the people that will be important for you to get to know, to build relationships, and those with whom you need to collaborate. I bring it up here as a check in. I encourage you, as part of your reflection, to pay particular attention to the relationships that you have built and those that you need to work on growing. People are the most important part of your work. In the matrixed world of healthcare delivery, so much of your success will be dependent on how well you manage relationships. The

Institute of Medicine's (IOM) report, "The Future of Nursing: Leading Change, Advancing Health," recommends that nurses be full partners with physicians and other healthcare professionals to lead improvement and redesign healthcare in the United States. As a leader in nursing, you cannot accomplish that without influence. Your sphere of influence needs to grow beyond your department. It needs to include areas outside of your direct control. You need to be influential with other professionals across disciplines. Relationships matter. Managing relationships is a competency to master. This competency is also called out in the AONL's Nurse Manager competency framework.

"The most important single ingredient in the formula of success is knowing how to get along with people." – Theodore Roosevelt, U.S. President

Paul Ryan, former speaker of the U.S. House of Representatives, once said, "Every successful individual knows that his or her achievement depends on a community of persons working together." Your ability to successfully manage relationships within your own department, across departments, with other disciplines and medical staff will drive your success. These relationships will come with conflict. Conflict should not be avoided and can actually strengthen a relationship when addressed. Reflect on how you are leading in this capacity. I encourage you to lean in and work to resolve issues when they arise. Start with the area of common ground – the purpose of care delivery or the patient. Listen to the other's perspective and objectively, share yours. Demonstrate your desire to help them be successful. Respect their role in the larger community of care providers, while maintaining a collaborative and collegial spirit. This will go a long way in building strong and productive relationships that will enable you to overcome challenges. Reflect on your relationships. Ask yourself:

- **Where are you building strong, productive relationships? How do you know?**

- **How are you leveraging your relationships to lead the business?**

- **How are you investing the right time in building relationships?**

- **What relationships have surprised you? Why?**

- **What relationships did you not build?**

- **Who (individuals or departments) deserve your gratitude?**

- **How have you remained curious about what you can learn from others?**

- **Where does conflict exist?**

- **How are you leading in conflict?**

Collaboration and teamwork are vital to the patient's experience. Your leadership will not support a collaborative environment if you are not building healthy relationships.

Leading the Development of Your Team

Throughout this book, I have discussed servant leadership and what it means. Servant leaders trust their team, provide guidance, empower their team and always look for opportunities to grow their skills and confidence. Take time to reflect on this aspect of your leadership. In the first three months as Nurse Manager, you assessed your team. As you move forward, be resolute, authentic and deliberate about how you will support their growth and development. Ken Blanchard and Mark Miller, in their book *The Secret*, discuss several aspects of great leaders. They suggest that the best leaders invest in the development of their people. They build an environment where people are so engaged that they dedicate themselves to helping achieve the vision. They create an expectation for learning and growing. Great leaders leverage the strengths of their team members and give them opportunities to develop their skills. They provide ongoing training and mentoring.

"The growth and development of people is the highest calling of leadership." – Harvey Firestone, Founder of Firestone Tire and Rubber Co

I understand that as a Nurse Manager, you likely have a large span of control with a large number of staff. Every associate is valuable, and each has their own development journey. It can be overwhelming when thinking about how to develop each individual. Start with team expectations and team performance. You will help individuals flourish when you foster team growth. You want your leadership to create the environment that individual team members foster the growth and development of one another. This comes from the expectations you establish and how your leadership demonstrates your values.

"The strength of the team is each member. The strength of each member is the team." – Phil Jackson, NBA player, coach & executive

From the start, being authentic you shared your core values and expectations. Your first three months were dedicated to really getting to know your team. As you reflect, what else can you discover that may lead to making some adjustments? The answers you come up with are the first steps to ensuring your effectiveness as a leader. Ask yourself:

- **Does your leadership reflect what you value and what you expect? What would others say?**

- **Does your leadership reflect the values of the organization? What would others say?**

- **How are you fostering teamwork and accountability? How do you know?**

- **How are you creating an engaging work environment? What do you notice?**

- **How do you know you have the right people on board? Where should you make changes?**

- **How are you continuing to help them develop?**

- **How can you ask and listen more before providing an answer?**

- **What does the team need from you?**

- **What do you need from the team?**

- **How can you support your team and the team support you as you lead the business?**

Earlier, in chapter six, I recommended that you focus first on those individuals who are in formal or informal leadership roles – those who are an extension of you. Your personal time and attention should focus first on the people you have entrusted to extend your leadership (i.e., committee leaders, charge nurses). Confirm that the right people are in these roles and that you are leveraging their leadership effectively. Give them your personal attention – mentor them and help them grow professionally. This will influence others. Their development will help you create the environment you desire. If you focus your attention elsewhere, you risk supporting poor behaviors by demonstrating tolerance of unaddressed conduct in these individuals.

As you reflect, consider how your leadership is influencing your team's development:

- **Have you created the structure for them to take more responsibility?**

- **How are you delegating decisions?**

- **How are you letting the team make decisions? How are you helping them own the decisions they make?**

- **How are you empowering them?**

- **How is your leadership hindering their empowerment?**

- **What else might you do to foster their empowerment?**

Remember, empowerment is both a process and an outcome that provides the ability to make effective and timely decisions. Empowering your team means providing the resources and creating the environment that supports decision-making. Empowerment, in your department, starts with your leadership. You need to create the structure, mentor the process, become a cheerleader and maintain the momentum that comes from empowerment. You need to deliberately reinforce activities and redirect when necessary. I mentioned strategies to engage your team embedded in previous sections. I discussed levels of authority and the PDSA cycle as ways to engage your team. All of these actions support an "ownership mentality" among your team, where individuals accept accountability for their own development and empowerment. It also benefits you. The more you empower your team, the more your team makes the decisions, the more they own, the less you have to manage and the more you can lead to the next level of performance. As you invest to support their development, you enhance their ability. Ronald Reagan once said, "the greatest leader is not necessarily the one who does the greatest things. He is the one that gets the people to do the greatest things." **How are you leveraging your team's talents to achieve great things?**

Lead Yourself

In the personal and professional turmoil of a transition, you have to intentionally maintain your equilibrium and preserve your ability to make good judgments. The risks of losing perspective, getting isolated and making bad calls are ever present during transitions. Skip Prichard's book, *The Book of Mistakes: 9 Secrets to Creating a Successful Future* is helpful as you reflect on your own inner dialogue that drives your behaviors. He wrote the book after interviewing more than 1,000 successful people. He captures several key lessons: 9 mistakes you should never make, 3 laws you should never break and 9 secrets to creating a successful future. Prichard describes common pitfalls that can trip us up. When I look back at my own leadership career, I see myself in many of the mistakes, and I encourage you to consider these in your reflection practice:

1. Working on someone else's dream – Even when your goals and accountabilities are defined by others, make the personal connection with your purpose and stay *resolute*. **Where do you need to create stronger connections to your purpose?**

2. Allowing someone else to define your value – You are more than a set of numbers or a title or your last interaction. Stay *authentic* to who you really are. **How are you honoring your inherent value?**

3. Accepting excuses – Be the "creator", the "challenger" or the "coach". Avoid playing the role of "victim" to your circumstances. Accept your authority because you are *empowered*. You own your next decision. Follow Florence Nightingale's example, "I attribute my success to this – I never gave or took any excuse." **What excuses are you making? What excuses are you allowing?**

4. Surrounding yourself with the wrong people – Pay attention to who you hang out with or go to lunch with. Be *deliberate* about surrounding yourself with individuals who foster your development. **Who are you spending time with? Do they help make you better?**

5. Staying in your comfort zone – Leading your team to a better future requires risk and potential failures. Lead them there anyway because you are *empowered*. **What challenges are you avoiding? What are you afraid of?**

6. Allowing temporary setbacks to become permanent failures – Celebrate the learning that comes from the failures. Stay *resolute* in your purpose, *inquisitive*, curious and move to the next try. **How are you celebrating failures?**

7. Trying to blend-in instead of standing out – Be true to who you are. You are *empowered* to follow your dreams. Alicia Keys once said, "You're stronger, you're better, and you're ready for whatever." Stay *resolute* and *authentic*. How **are you standing out? Where are you holding yourself back? How are you letting your unique light shine?**

8. Thinking that there is a "fixed" or "limited" amount of success available – Focusing on what you cannot have or do is scarcity thinking. Focus instead on the infinite possibilities available to you. Stay *resolute, deliberate,* and *inquisitive,* you are *empowered.* **What limitations are you experiencing? What possibilities exist to overcome them?**

9. Believing you have all the time in the world – Prioritize and focus on the important things, act with urgency and with *deliberate* action. **What are you putting off in order to deal with less urgent issues? How can you empower your team to reduce time spent solving their problems?**

Add Prichard's book to your must-have list. It is a unique look at what derails us as leaders. It can be helpful as you build habits to overcome them. Explore the mistakes, the laws and the secrets to success as you reflect and make adjustments. Your wellbeing will be enhanced and you will feel more empowered.

In chapter three I suggested you download the AONL Nurse Manager Competencies as a guide to your development as you grow in the role. Take a look at them now as you are reflecting. **How are you progressing with the competencies outlined? Where do you**

want to focus more? How can you leverage your current challenges to grow in the competencies identified?

"Self-care is not a luxury. Indeed not. It allows us to show up in this tumultuous world as the best versions of ourselves." – Unknown

Practice Self-care – Earlier, I shared about an instance when I found myself in a vicious cycle, and a mentor told me to be "appropriately selfish." My mentor wanted me to realize that I was not spending enough time reflecting on my own leadership. I was focused on others – my resilience was depleted and I was not being effective. He wanted me to see the impact of my leadership from a more objective point of view. Being "appropriately selfish" is a concept that many nurses grapple with (I sure did). Although we often teach this to our patients, we are not great at practicing this in our own lives. As a leader, I urge you to set the example. Demonstrate healthy behaviors. Demonstrate your willingness to change and grow as you learn to become a more effective leader. Take care of you and your development as you care for and develop others. Be the role model.

To this day, I grapple with the contradiction of caring for oneself in terms of servant leadership. I am a firm believer in servant leadership, and I know that I cannot effectively do what I need to do if I do not spend time tending to myself. In a video titled, "Who Comes First: You or the Group?" Simon Sinek addresses the difficulty behind the struggle. He says that it is simply a paradox to being human. He discusses the debate between us as individuals and us as group members. He shares, "Some believe we should always put others first, that if we don't look out for the group, the group will not look out for us. Others believe we should always put ourselves first, and that if we don't take care of ourselves first, then we would be of no use to anyone else. The fact is both are true." He acknowledges the difficulty and daily struggle we experience. Both are important. You will make decisions everyday choosing between the two. If you demonstrate one always being more important than the other (always choosing the same one priority over the other) you will fail to create the culture you want. You must role model choosing between the two priorities effectively, sometimes choosing your team over yourself and sometimes choosing yourself over the team. I have found that self-awareness and situational awareness can effectively help you make the choice. The *15 Commitments to Conscious Leadership* helped me with this paradox. When I shifted my paradigm to helping others become radically aware and responsible, it forced me to consider this in a healthier way.

"Please place the mask over your own mouth and nose before assisting others." Many of us have heard these words before, but how often do we pause to think about the significance of this philosophy when we need it most? This phrase is more than white noise as an airplane gets ready to take off, it is an effective way to help others. Mary Koloroutis, in *Relationship Based Care*, discusses three critical relationships to the caregiver: the relationship with the patient, the relationship with colleagues and the relationship with ourselves. Each is vital to the provision of care. All three relationships must be balanced. Too often, we neglect that relationship with ourselves. We need energy to effectively lead. As humans, we only have a finite amount of energy to operate – taking care of ourselves helps replenish our energy. Refilling our tank is not selfish, it is essential to effectively lead. Refilling your tank is not selfish if done to support your purpose of caring for others. Tending to your own needs will make you better equipped to support others. Self-care builds capacity and personal strength, it brings out the best in you, and enables you to give more of yourself.

You are navigating through a challenging time with significant pressure to make an impact. Your team, boss and patients depend on you. You are also depending on you. Amidst all you do, it is incredibly important that you are tending to your own energy. Self-care is not selfish. Your wellbeing and resilience are indispensable to your effective leadership. First, you need to maintain an energy level that enables you to effectively lead. Second you need to demonstrate a healthy balance of caring for self to care for others. **How are you caring for yourself?** Reflect on your own strength, energy and enthusiasm. **What is your energy level like? How do you refill your tank? Are you refilling your tank often enough?**

Grow your self-reflection skill. Build a habit of reflecting in the moment. Strategically schedule uninterrupted think time dedicated to reflect, learn and adjust. Through the reflection of your leadership, relationships, your team's development and your own resilience, you will find ways to enable and encourage others more effectively. Taking time dedicated to reflection will enable you to accelerate the changes that you want to make – improvement in your influence, improvement in your relationships, improvement in tactics, improvement in decision-making, improvement in your leadership. Reflection will help you hone your *READI* leadership attributes to be the best you possible.

"Without reflection, we go blindly on our way, creating more unintended consequences, and failing to achieve anything useful." –

Margaret Wheatley, author, teacher, speaker, &
management consultant

Make Adjustments

Your uninterrupted reflection time should include consideration for adjustments to be made to enhance your effectiveness Use all of the feedback you have received and the insights from your own reflection to determine what to adjust. Identify any destructive behaviors that are holding you back. Consider your own vulnerabilities and how to compensate for them. Put this learning into action and determine how you will shift your action plans, tactics and leadership to manage the environment and foster success. As you work through this process, ascertain how your own leadership may need to change, what relationships may need work, how to further develop your team and how to successfully lead yourself. Once you identify learnings and make decisions about your leadership, let your boss know what you plan to do. Let your colleagues know. Let your team know. Ask your boss, your team and your colleagues for ongoing feedback.

Start Stop Continue

One of my favorite tools for getting and distilling feedback into an action-oriented plan is the "start, stop, continue" model, also known as the "stop, keep, start" (SKS) model. Phil Daniels, a Brigham Young University psychology professor, developed this model. This tool will help you organize your reflection learning and the feedback received in order to take action and evolve your leadership. **What should you start doing, stop doing and continue doing?** A slight variation is KISS – "what to keep, what to improve, what to start and what to stop doing." Harvard Business School professor, Thomas Delong suggests that, "knowing what we should quit, continue, and start doing anchors us in reality." This tool is simple, practical and can be leveraged in multiple ways. It is a great way to solicit feedback by simply asking others what you should start, stop and continue to be more effective. I have used this tool in conversations with my own boss, with colleagues and with subordinates. I have used this tool in team settings, during performance appraisals, facilitating discussions with teams to improve team functioning, redesign processes and in evaluating action plans.

The start/stop/continue model is self-explanatory. Identify that which would be helpful to start, that which is harmful and must stop, and that which has worked and should continue.

Although a simple concept, knowing what is important to continue while taking action on what to start and stop can be challenging. Some will be easy to discern and deploy, but others will be more problematic. Be resolute and courageous. In *Flying Without a Net*, DeLong emphasizes the courage it takes to make these kinds of changes. He discusses how we need to draw strength from our vulnerability by learning and addressing our challenges. Apply the start/stop/continue exercise to the tactics you are deploying to improve outcomes. Apply it to your relationships with your team, your colleagues the medical staff and your boss. Apply it to your own leadership as you lead and grow your team. Apply it to how you lead yourself.

Using the tool, you will identify what you want to adjust as you lead forward. In chapter three I discussed several tactics to help you prepare. I discussed the concept of "what got you here won't get you there." This concept applies here as well. As a leader, you must be willing to constantly evolve your leadership. You must be willing to evolve and grow. A coach once told me that unless you are uncomfortable you are not growing. As humans we seek the comfort zone. Your leadership, however, demands you get uncomfortable. Unless we are willing to get uncomfortable and evolve our leadership, we will not achieve our aspirations. It will take resolute courage to take action and make the improvements you want to make. DeLong suggests that we should courageously "do the right things poorly" so that we can do "the right things well." In other words, to effectively adjust, we must be willing to try new things, be open to experiment and willing to fail as we practice new skills. Through the awkwardness of learning new skills, we will come to do the right things well.

"We can't become what we need to be by remaining what we are." – Oprah Winfrey, talk show host, actress, philanthropist

Stay resolute in your purpose and the leader you wish to be. You are empowered to do what is right. As you authentically review what you should start, stop and continue, you may discover destructive behaviors that need to change. Be deliberate. It will take vulnerability as you adjust your leadership and deploy new tactics and decisions. Keep a learning mindset and stay inquisitive about the impact of your leadership. Stay *READI* as you carry on, reflecting, adjusting and executing your leadership.

6 Months: Reflect & Adjust

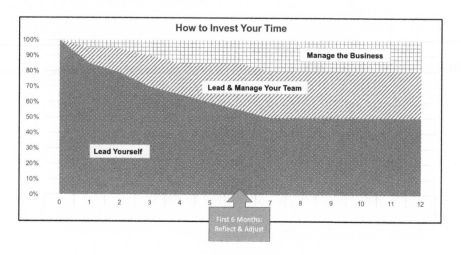

Actions to take:

✓ Manage your calendar

    – Further deploy your visibility plan

    – Continue to progress through your relationship heat map

    – Continue to check off the processes you are learning and doing independently

    – Schedule an uninterrupted day for reflection and planning

✓ Answer the questions in bold font to help your self-reflection and planning

✓ Apply start/stop/continue to your plan, relationships and leadership

✓ Identify and implement adjustments to grow and empower your team

✓ Identify and implement adjustments enhance strong, collaborative relationships

✓ Identify and implement identified adjustments to your plans to achieve better results

✓ Delegate authority where and when you can

✓ Build a habit to reflect as part of your daily routines – share key learning with your boss, colleagues and team

✓ Start a decision journal and a thought diary

✓ Start a mindfulness meditation practice

✓ Practice self-care

Tools shared:

✓ Decision Journal

✓ Thought Diary

✓ Start/Stop/Continue

Must haves for your library:

✓ *The Book of Mistakes: 9 Secrets to Creating a Successful Future* by Skip Prichard – it will provide insights into your behavior and help you avoid common pitfalls.

Quick tip hints for your success:

✓ Review the IOM's report, *The Future of Nursing: Leading Change, Advancing Health.* This will give you insight regarding our profession, as well as actions that can be used to leverage the largest professional group within the health care industry.

✓ Ask your team and colleagues how you can be a better leader. Ask them what you should start, stop and continue doing. Incorporate their feedback as you make adjustments. Let them know how you are taking action based on their feedback.

CHAPTER EIGHT

12 Months: Grow Your Leadership

As you finish the first six months and look to the second six months of your first year, you will continue growing your leadership capacity as you grow the competencies required in your role. Leading in your role as Nurse Manager, you have many priorities. The skills required to expertly lead are numerous. The focus of the next six months is to grow your effectiveness, grow your influence, and make an impact as you continue to lead your team. The role of Nurse Manager requires following methodical and deliberate processes to manage the business, manage relationships and manage your team. Your success in the role requires thoughtful, empowered, authentic and resolute leadership to provide the guidance your team needs to excel. In addition to integrating the content already discussed, I will focus on developing your skills and expanding your influence to prepare for the next six months. I will share additional theory, tools and tactics to more effectively lead yourself, lead your team and manage the business. Throughout each area consider your resolute focus on purpose, your empowered initiative, your authentic self, your deliberate actions and your inquiring spirit. Note how your *READI* leadership is integrated.

Lead Yourself

> *"Leadership is not about a title or a designation. It's about impact, influence, and inspiration."* – Robin S. Sharma, writer, motivational speaker

Your effectiveness as a leader starts with an understanding of who you are, who you want to be and what you want to achieve. Lead yourself so you can let your light shine and inspire the light in others. Over the last three months, you have taken time to reflect, evaluate your leadership and make adjustments. This is a cycle that you will continue throughout your career. In order to be most effective for the teams that you lead, teams you are a part of, and leaders you report to, you need to continually advance your leadership through reflection, learning and adjustment. Dee Hock, founder and former CEO of the VISA Credit Card Association once said, "Control is not leadership; management is not leadership; leadership is leadership. If you seek to lead, invest at least 50 percent of your time in leading yourself, your own purpose, ethics, principles, motivation, conduct. Invest at least 20 percent leading those with authority over you and 15 percent leading your peers." According to him, that leaves only 15 percent to lead your team. That doesn't seem like enough right? The first time I heard this my jaw dropped. I just could not fathom the time breakdown he suggested. I dismissed it almost immediately. What I have come to realize is that Hock was more right than wrong. Effectively leading requires effective leadership of self first. As you continue this first year as Nurse Manager, continue to focus on leading yourself. It is easy to get lost in all of the other priorities around you. Leading yourself will help you be more effective in so many other aspects of your responsibilities. Leading yourself means owning your development, taking initiative to learn and grow and managing. It requires self-awareness, self-discipline and self- regulation. It requires that you put into practice to behaviors to manage yourself. When you are successful at leading yourself, you will take responsibility for your behavior, you will act with integrity, and you will gain credibility and influence.

Learn and Grow

Throughout this book, I have discussed your development and offered up areas for you to learn and grow. The purpose of this book is your development. Building the habit to invest in your own development is essential as a professional and as leader. Think about development using the 70/20/10 guideline – 70% of your development should be "on-the-job" learning by working; 20% learning through interactions with other leaders, mentors, coaches and peers; and 10% from formal training. As an adult learner, your experiences are a significant resource for learning. The information is more relevant, there is greater context, and it enables you to integrate the learning for sustained growth. The most powerful of adult learning comes from our experiences and the ability to integrate new information and skills immediately, hence the 70+20%; learning by doing with the assistance of others to integrate the learning through conversation and reflection to foster understanding. My mother used to always say, "When the learner is ready, the teacher will appear." Personally, the teacher has taken many shapes and sizes for me – bosses, peers, mentors, coaches, articles I have read, seemingly insignificant conversations I've had with others, and activities in which I have participated. Remarkably, although I may have heard or been exposed to the information previously, this teacher appeared when I was most able to integrate and use it. And in most cases the teacher appeared in the normal course of my day. **How have teachers shown up for you? How have you embraced the learning opportunities that exist in your daily activities?**

The important thing is that you own your development. Don't let barriers be an excuse to your own progression. You own seeking new information to grow your awareness and understanding. If you do not understand something, you have the ability to ask, read and discover. You own your decisions and decision-making. You are empowered. The spirit with which you embrace that ownership, the intention you put into learning will drive your success. The reflective practice shared in chapter seven, once integrated into your daily routines will provide opportunity for powerful development. As you consider in the moment what went well, what could have gone better and how you contributed to the outcome, you will be making powerful discoveries every day. Ralph Waldo Emerson said, "Men succeed when they realize that their failures are the preparation for their victories." Take advantage of learning every day. Be intentional about learning through any experience. It is through this learning that we are able to do the things we were once not able to do. It provides the opportunity to evaluate our strengths and weaknesses, then we can take action leveraging our strengths to manage our weaknesses. Lead your own life – set your course, follow it and correct it as you go.

"Be patient with yourself. Self-growth is tender; it's holy ground. There's no greater investment." – Stephen Covey, educator, author, keynote speaker

In addition, take advantage of the formal learning opportunities that exist in your organization. Get involved in professional organizations, subscribe and read journals, pursue additional formal academic education, attend professional conferences and plan to become certified. Each of these opportunities provide for unique learning for your development. To be most effective, make a habit of integrating what you learn in these formal settings immediately. Earning credentialed letters and contact hours do not equal development. Growth occurs when learning is integrated into your practice; when your thoughts and behavior change, only then are you developing. The courage to integrate learning is what enables us to overcome our fears and do more. In the words of Henry Ford, "One of the greatest discoveries a man makes, one of his greatest surprises, is to find he can do what he was afraid he couldn't."

Development is a life-long journey. The habit of consistently growing your own knowledge, skills and abilities must occur before you can support the same for others. I referenced the AONL Nurse Manager Competencies previously. In chapter three I suggested that you download and use it as a guide for the skills that need to be developed. Again, in chapter seven I suggested you review it as part of your reflection. The document can serve as a checklist to your ongoing development. It will serve as a resource should you desire certification in the practice of nursing leadership (both AONL and ANCC have certifications for you to consider). Throughout the remainder of your first year in the Nurse Manager Role (and throughout your career) be deliberate about your professional development. Model the way to be a lifelong learner. You truly can't develop others if you're not spending time developing yourself. The benefit – you grow as a person and as a professional, you improve your self-awareness, you boost your confidence and grow your leadership capacity, you will inspire others to grow.

"There is no end to education. It is not that you read a book, pass an examination, and finish with education. The whole of life, from the moment you are born to the moment you die, is a process of learning." – Jiddu Krishnamurti, philosopher, speaker and writer

Self-Awareness, Self-Discipline, Self-Regulation

Self-regulation refers to our ability to monitor and manage our emotions, thoughts and behaviors in a way that produces positive results such as learning, maintaining strong relationships and improved wellbeing. Self-discipline is the ability to control our thoughts and feelings in order to control our behavior and overcome our weaknesses. It enables us to pursue goals through difficulties and control ourselves without outside direction. Self-awareness is the experience of one's own individuality and humanness. It involves being aware of different aspects of the self, including our traits, emotions, feelings and the triggers to our behaviors. Self-awareness enables self-discipline, which enables self-regulation. Our ability to self-regulate behavior in spite of our inner dialogue empowers us to act with courage, see other perspectives and be more accepting. It produces stronger relationships. It fosters creativity, innovation and better problem solving.

Self-awareness has been woven throughout each section of this book. As stated previously, self-awareness is a key ingredient to exceptional leadership. In her *Harvard Business Review* article, Tasha Eurich, PhD, an organizational psychologist, researcher, and *New York Times* bestselling author, writes "Research suggests that when we see ourselves clearly, we are more confident and more creative. We make sounder decisions, build stronger relationships, and communicate more effectively. We're less likely to lie, cheat, and steal. We are better workers who get more promotions. And we're more effective leaders with more satisfied employees." How do you become more self-aware? A self-assessment as suggested in chapter three and the reflective practices shared in chapter seven are examples to help you grow self-awareness. In addition, our bodies can tell us a great deal if we pay attention to them. We often feel physical sensations before we are able to acknowledge an emotion. Lauri Nummenmaaa, Enrico Glereana, Riitta Harib, and Jari Hietanen share their research on this subject in their article, "Bodily Maps of Emotions" in the official journal of the Proceedings of the National Academy of Sciences (PNAS). Through their research, the authors mapped somatic sensations with emotions. They concluded that emotional feelings are associated with discrete bodily sensations. Nummenmaaa and her colleagues suggest that understanding the bodily sensations associated with human emotions will help us better understand our emotional energy. For example, we feel love generalized throughout our core, chest and head. We feel sadness in the center of our chest over our heart. We feel anger in our upper body, neck and head. We feel anxiety in our abdomen and chest. Picking up on the subtle sensations fosters awareness and then enables us to regulate our response to situations. These sensations hold true across gender, ethnicity and culture. Search "emotion body mapping" on the internet to see the full array of emotions mapped. Use your physical sensations as a key to explore your emotions. Pay attention to what you are experiencing, what you are feeling (emotionally and physically) and what you are thinking. This insight will give you the feedback necessary to decipher your emotions, explore your thinking, and regulate your behavior to be disciplined and lead from a place of consciousness. **What can you discover by paying attention to your**

physical sensations? How do your physical sensations correspond with your emotions?

Accepting accountability and taking responsibility are key to self-discipline and self-regulation.

It requires owning our behavior and accepting responsibility for it. Lead with integrity and accept accountability for the behaviors you exhibit and the decisions you make. Courtney Lynch one of the authors of the book *Spark: How to Lead Yourself and Others to Greater Success* wrote, "Leaders inspire accountability through their ability to accept responsibility before they place blame." When you take responsibility rather than place blame, you inspire confidence in your leadership. The vulnerability you show by owning your own behavior including mistakes, demonstrates it is OK to get it wrong occasionally. You will inspire accountability in others.

"Everything can be taken from a man but one thing: the last of the human freedoms – to choose one's attitude in any given set of circumstances." – Viktor Frankl, Holocaust survivor

In chapter one, I mentioned conscious leadership as the evolution of servant leadership. Conscious leaders are radically aware of their thinking that drives their behavior in order to become radically responsible for how they regulate their behavior. In The 15 *Commitments of Conscious* Leadership the authors provide great guidance for self-awareness, self-discipline and self-regulation. Practicing the commitments outlined fosters curiosity, learning, integrity and accountability. Conscious leadership asks us to become more truthful with ourselves and others. It requires us to be authentic and take responsibility for our interactions. According to Dethmer, unconscious leaders are reactive. He states, "They react from a 'story' about the past or an imagined future, and their personality, ego, or mind takes over." Practicing conscious leadership enables us to lead with a high degree of awareness. We bring our better selves to the situation verses the reactive lesser version of ourselves. We take on the role of a coach, helping others to learn verses the role of hero where we rescue or "just do it ourselves." We take on the role of a challenger placing healthy pressure on ourselves and others to change verses a villain placing blame. We take on the role of creator, owning our circumstances verses being a victim to our circumstances. Increasing your consciousness will help you accept who you are, accept accountability for behaviors you exhibit and decisions you make. It will help you create an environment of trust. It will help you foster stronger relationships and grow your influence. Your self-awareness, self-regulation and self-discipline will enhance your understanding of your resolute purpose, it will empower you, it will grow your authenticity, it will provide insight to be more deliberate, it will ignite your spirit of inquiry. With greater awareness you will maximize your leadership impact.

"The greatness of a man is not in how much wealth he acquires but, in his integrity, and in his ability to affect those around him positively." – Bob Marley, singer, songwriter, musician

Manage Yourself

Successfully leading yourself will require you to organize and control yourself. The self-discipline and self-regulation discussed in the previous section will support your ability to control yourself. In addition, you need to be deliberate to manage your activities to that you can accomplish everything on your "to-do" list. Act deliberately.

Take steps to organize your calendar and make good use of your time. Regulate yourself and build the habits that help you be your best self. Monitor your wellbeing and manage your resilience.

"Things that matter most must not be at the mercy of things that matter least." – Johann Wolfgang von Goethe, 18th century scientist, statesman, poet & playwright

Manage Your Time – Albert Einstein said, "The only reason for time is so that everything doesn't happen at once." Time is finite and is our most precious resource. You cannot do everything at once and everything takes time. Stephen Covey famously said, "The key is not spending time, but investing it." Great leaders are deliberate about how they invest their time. Commit time to processes that allow you to be proactive and do things more quickly and easily. In their *Harvard Business Review* article, "Beware the Busy Manager," Heike Bruch and Sumantra Ghoshal share that after a decade of research, they determined that only 10% of managers spent time in a committed and purposeful way, while 90% of managers squandered their time on ineffective activities. William Oncken and Donald L Wass, in another *Harvard Business Review* article, "Who's Got the Monkey?" discuss three different types of time imposed on leaders: boss-imposed time, system-imposed time and self-imposed time:

- Boss-imposed time is used to accomplish those activities that your boss (or the organization) requires. You cannot disregard these without penalty. Plan for these on your calendar and dedicate prep time as necessary.

- System-imposed time is used to accommodate requests from peers for active support. Neglecting these requests may hurt relationships. Be aware of what you say "yes" to and what you commit to.

- Self-imposed time is used to do the things that you originate or agree to do. Subordinates will use a certain portion of this time (called subordinate-imposed time). The remaining portion is "discretionary time."

Your goal is to increase your discretionary time. Oncken and Wass contend that leaders often commit too much time accepting responsibility for things that should remain in their subordinates' (or others) hands. They use the analogy of a monkey to illustrate their point. Imagine a conversation with a team member. During the discussion they share a concern; you have ideas on how it can be resolved. There are two choices, 1) to coach them in resolving the concern for themselves or 2) to take responsibility for resolving it yourself. When you accept the responsibility yourself, you take the monkey from your team member and put it on your own back. Doing so, you accept responsibility for the care and feeding of that monkey. One monkey is not so bad – **how often do you walk down the hall accepting monkeys from multiple individuals?** Care and feeding of the monkeys take time; time that could be used in more constructive ways. Be cautious about what you accept that does not require you or your position of authority to complete. **Are you carrying monkeys? How could you work with your team and colleagues to not accept their monkeys?**

In another *Harvard Business Review* article, "Manage Your Energy, Not Your Time," Tony Schwartz and Catherine McCarthy suggest paying attention to our energy. We can be more efficient when we focus on energy first: "The core problem with working longer hours is that time is a finite resource. Energy is a different story." Schwartz and McCarthy review where energy comes from and suggest activities to enhance the energy through our body, emotions, mind and spirit. According to their research, focusing on energy and energy renewal will increase your capacity.

- Body – exercise, pay attention to your nutrition, sleep, take lunch breaks, walk for brief periods of time and go outside when you can

- Emotions –deep breathing, showing gratitude, alternative thinking and changing your story (see the discussion about self-awareness above)

- Mind – avoid distractions, do not read emails when you are tending to other tasks, manage interruptions, close your office door, focus for short periods of time, be proactive with larger, challenging tasks, break large tasks into smaller ones and schedule accordingly

- Spirit – we tap into this energy when our everyday work is consistent with what we value most and what gives us a meaning and purpose. Find the connections in the mission and values of the organization.

Based on their study, Schwartz and McCarthy found that 71% of participants of a structured program focused on building energy had a noticeable or substantial positive impact on their productivity and performance. **What habits should you start to shift your energy to help build leadership capacity?**

"We live in deed, not years; In thoughts not breaths; In feelings, not figures on a dial. We should count time by heart throbs." – Aristotle

Manage your calendar to best invest your time and enable you to spend time on the important things that you need to spend time doing. Schedule tasks to complete them on time. Schedule time proactively to work on those tasks that have deadlines. Be disciplined about your visibility plan and manage your calendar accordingly. Take caution accepting ownership for tasks that others have the ability to complete. Spend time on things that give you energy. Deliberately manage your time. Be intentional so you can be effective.

Tend to Yourself – In chapter seven, I discussed the need to care for yourself. It is discussed again here as an important aspect of leading and managing yourself. You cannot be the leader you desire to be if you lack the energy required to lead. You must manage your energy supply. We often take for granted our fuel to thrive – our capacity to work is our energy. Fueling our energy will allow us to be better leaders, get more done and be more effective. Be deliberate about your wellbeing and your resilience. The following practices will help grow your energy supply:

- Practice deep breathing – taking a deep breath and a long exhale lowers your heart rate and your blood pressure. It has a positive impact on your immune system and improves your sleep. Practice taking a deep breath in through your nose counting to four, exhale through your mouth counting to six. Completing just four to six cycles can have an incredible calming effect. This is something easily done throughout your day.

- Practice savoring – savoring is the act of appreciating positive moments. Deliberately focusing on pleasant feelings allows us to stay present in the "here and now," even if for just a moment. It helps us remember the "good stuff." Take a deep breath and a moment to appreciate the sunset, the smell of cookies, the giggle of a baby, the fact that the elevator went directly to your floor or you found a parking spot close to the door. Savor the connection you witness between an associate and their patient. Savor a moment when you see associates working well together. Find the moments to savor – they are all around you.

- Practice gratitude – the simple act of showing gratitude can improve your mood, strengthen your immune system, lower your stress level and blood pressure. It fosters stronger social connection. Write down what you are grateful for, snap a quick photo of something that you appreciate. Write thank you notes. Reflect on what you savored today and be grateful.

- Do a Random Act of Kindness – the act of showing kindness like savoring improves your mood, lowers your stress, strengthen your immune system and lowers blood pressure. It fosters stronger social connection. Buy a cup of coffee for the person behind you in line, offer to turn a patient for one of your staff members, take a peer out for a walk and tell them what they mean to you. Try to do at least one random act of kindness every day.

- Make Social Connections – Social interactions make us happier and can significantly improve our mood. Call a friend or schedule lunch with someone you have not seen in a while. Smile and say hello to the people you meet as you walk through the halls. Talk to the cashier when you buy a cup of coffee or the person bagging your groceries.

- Exercise – The benefits of exercise are numerous. There are the obvious physical benefits as well as improving mood, mental acuity, and decreasing depressive symptoms. If you already have an exercise routine, keep it up. If not, find 15 minutes a couple of times a week to walk.

- Sleep – Getting adequate sleep is essential to brain function. It helps with improving mood and cognitive performance. It decreases risk of heart disease, diabetes and cancer. Track your sleep and try to get 6-8 hours a night. You will be more effective.

- Meditate – Through meditation, we can control our mind from wandering and become more present in the moment. Meditation can improve your mood, decrease stress and improve cognitive ability. If you already meditate, keep doing it. If not, start with a five-minute meditation. There are several apps that can help you get started.

Be resolute in managing your wellbeing, you are empowered to take action. Authentically savor the 'good stuff', show gratitude and build relationships. Take deliberate action, write a thank you note, journal, exercise and get some sleep. Learn to meditate. Stay inquisitive, discover the benefits as you build the skills discussed. **What habits should you start to enhance your wellbeing and grow your leadership capacity?**

Build Positive Habits – To better lead and manage yourself you need to build new habits. Our habits become who we are. Building new habits can be difficult because there is comfort in old ways of thinking. When we are stressed, we lean toward our "comfort zone." Leading requires deliberate focus on incorporating new behavior into your routines, for yourself and others. Building a new habit requires the motivation to change, the courage to change and the discipline to consistently practice the changed behavior. Gabrielle Oettingen has been studying the impact of dreams on motivation since the early 1990s. In her book, *Rethinking Positive Thinking*, she introduces the four-step WOOP (Wish, Outcome, Obstacle, Plan) method. The WOOP method is based on research and years of scientific studies. It is easy to learn and apply. It is based on mental contrasting which is a self-regulation strategy. Oettingen suggests that when you experience the contrast between where you want to be and where you are, it brings forth a motivation to take action. She suggests, "it's making the most of our fantasies by brushing them up against the very thing most of us are taught to ignore or diminish: the obstacles that stand in our way."

Use WOOP to build new habits:

1. WISH – Create a wish. What habit do you want to start? Be specific and describe it in 3-6 words.

2. OUTCOME – Envision the outcome. What is the benefit that you may experience as a result of achieving the wish? Briefly describe it, by being clear and specific.

3. OBSTACLES – Identify the obstacles that you will realistically face. What obstacle(s) will you create that would prevent you

from making your wish come true? What other obstacle(s) may get in your way? First, focus on the internal, self-created obstacles. Identify as many as possible. Prioritize them and rank them by likelihood and significance.

4. PLAN – Create a plan to address your obstacles. What will you do to manage the most significant obstacles you identified? Make an "If (*_obstacle_*) then I will (*_plan_*)" chart to identify your actions. Identify the most effective path you can take for each obstacle.

Envision the possibilities of what could be true and face the challenges with a deliberate and thoughtful plan. Be *READI*.

"We are what we repeatedly do. Excellence then, is not an act, but a habit."
– Aristotle

Lead And Manage Your Team

Throughout this book, I have discussed theory, shared some research, tools and tactics to help you lead your team. The people on your team are your most important asset. Your success is accomplished through their work. There are systems and processes that you need to deliberately manage in order for your team to successfully accomplish their work. You need to ensure the correct staffing plan; you need to ensure the right number of positions are filled and scheduled to provide the right level of care. You need to interview and hire effectively. You need to develop and deploy strategies to retain team members. You need to address performance and promote ongoing development of individuals as you bring the individuals together as a team. All require the art of leadership as you effectively manage each.

Staff Planning

The success of your department is contingent on having the right number of people doing the right things. You need to establish the correct staffing plan. Start at the core – at the point of care and identify the number and type of staff required on each shift based on the typical volume of patients needing care. Determine if and how much volume varies by day of week and time of day. Once you have a core number, determine the mix of full-time, part-time and per diem associates to manage the fluctuations in volume and cover the schedule. Determine the right blend for each shift and every season. Your organization may have a standard for weekend and holiday rotations Determine if or how this may impact the number or mix of associates you need. Understanding the answers to these questions will help you determine the number and type of positions you need to have filled. In addition, your staffing plan needs to follow your budgeted or allocated labor resources. **Does your plan enable the department to work within the allocated budget?** If you discover a discrepancy, clarify with your boss and make the necessary changes to the staffing plan based on what patients need, staying within the allocated budget. If you cannot meet patient needs within the budgeted resources, build your case and share with your boss. Plan to make a request for additional resources.

I will be taking you through an example, however be sure to investigate the staff planning tools used at your organization. Follow your organizations process. Here's the example: Consider that you are the manager of a 24-bed inpatient unit. The average daily census is 20. The census typically dips over the weekend. Mid-week, patient volume is closer to 23-24 and on weekends is 16-18. Patient volume fluctuates throughout the day, with more patients on the unit during the day than at night. Team members work 12-hour shifts and your plan includes a 1:5 nurse to patient ratio and a 1:12 aid to patient ratio. Full-time team members work three 12-hr shifts/week. The standard in your organization requires staff to work every third weekend. Make a grid and identify the number and type of staff needed at each census level:

Patient Volume	Day	Night
24	5 RNs - 2 aids	5 RNs - 2 aids
23	5 RNs - 2 aids	5 RNs - 2 aids
22	5 RNs - 2 aids	5 RNs - 2 aids
21	5 RNs - 2 aids	5 RNs - 2 aids
20	4 RNs - 2 aids	4 RNs - 2 aids
19	4 RNs - 2 aids	4 RNs - 2 aids
18	4 RNs - 2 aids	4 RNs - 2 aids
17	4 RNs - 2 aids	4 RNs - 1 aid
16	4 RNs - 1 aid	4 RNs - 1 aid
15	3 RNs - 1 aid	3 RNs - 1 aid
14	3 RNs - 1 aid	3 RNs - 1 aid

Make a schedule grid. For this example, you need to create a template that includes three weeks given every third weekend standard. Start with the weekends and fill in the weekend staffing requirements. Based on the typical weekend volume you will need 4 RNs and 2 aids. With the volume higher mid-week, you should plan for 5 RNs and 2 aids on Tuesdays, Wednesdays and Thursdays.

Volume grows throughout the day on Monday, to accommodate this, plan for 5 RNs and 2 aids. The volume drops throughout the day on Fridays, so plan for 5 RNs and 2 aids during the days and 4 RNs and 2 aids at night.

		S	M	T	W	T	F	S	S	M	T	W	T	F	S	S	M	T	W	T	F	S
Day	RN	4	5	5	5	5	5	4	4	5	5	5	5	5	4	4	5	5	5	5	5	4
Day	Aid	2	2	2	2	2	2	2	2	2	2	2	2	2	2	2	2	2	2	2	2	2
Night	RN	4	5	5	5	5	4	4	4	5	5	5	5	4	4	4	5	5	5	5	4	4
Night	Aid	2	2	2	2	2	2	2	2	2	2	2	2	2	2	2	2	2	2	2	2	2

This plan requires 33 RN 7am-7pm (day) shifts to be covered/week and 28 RN 7pm-7am (night) shifts/week; 14 7am-7pm (day) aid shifts/week and 14 7pm-7am (night) aid shifts/week.

- To cover the weekend RN needs, with team members working every third weekend, you need a minimum of 12 RN positions (4x3) dedicated to each shift. If each of them works 3 shifts a week, that provides 36-day shifts and 36 night shifts. (I will discuss benefit time in a moment)

- To cover the weekend aid needs, you need 6 individual aid positions (2x3) dedicated to each shift. If each of them works 3 shifts a week, that provides 18 day shifts and 18 night shifts each week.

- Apply the same process for the aid positions

Now, you have to plan for benefit time and flexibility. Every staff member will take time off and you need to plan for routine time off as well as further fluctuations in volume. Determine the average benefit time on your department. For this example, we will use a 15% as the benefit time, meaning that 15% of an associate's time is paid time off. Identify the right mix of full and part-time that works for the department – you do not want 100% of your team working full-time. A general guide to start with is to use the 70-80% working full time. You can always change the mix of full time to part time as you learn more.

Calculate worked and benefit FTE required (1 FTE works 40 hours/week):

- 33 RN day shifts/week = 9.9 FTEs (33 shifts x 12 hours per shift / 40 hours per FTE); 28 RN night shifts/week = 8.4 FTEs (28 x 12 / 40). Add benefit time to calculate total paid FTE required – 9.9 + 15% = 11.4 RN FTEs on days; 8.4 + 15% = 9.7 RN FTEs on nights.

- 14 Aid day shifts/week = 4.2 FTEs (14 x 12/40); 14 Aid day shifts/week = 4.2 FTEs (14 x 12/40). Add benefit time to calculate total paid FTE required (4.2 + 15% = 0.6) – add 0.6 FTE to both shifts, total of 5 Aid FTEs on each shift.

- The staffing plan in this example requires:

  – 11.4 RN FTEs dedicated to working day shifts

  – RN FTEs dedicated to working night shifts

  – 5 Aid FTEs dedicated to working day shift

— 5 Aid FTEs dedicated to working night shift

Brush off your algebra skills and convert the FTEs required to the number of positions needed Positions are always whole numbers – round up; there is some art and improvisation required as you work through this conversion. In this example you will need:

- 14 RNs on day shift: 10 full-time (10 x 0.9 = 9.0 FTEs) and 4 part-time (4 x 0.6 = 2.4 FTEs); 9.0 FTEs + 2.4 FTEs = 11.4 FTEs (11.4 FTE is required)

- 12 RNs on night shift, 8 full-time (9 x 0.9 = 8.1 FTEs) and 3part-time (3 x 0.6 = 1.8 FTEs); 8.1 FTEs + 1.8 FTEs = 9.9 FTEs (9.7 FTE is required)

- Total of 26 RN positions; 19 full-time and 7 part-time

- 6 Aid positions on each shift, 5 full-time (5 x 0.9 = 4.5 FTEs) and 1 part-time (1 x 0.6 = 0.6 FTE); 4.5 FTE + 0.6 FTE = 5.1 FTE for each shift (5.0 FTE required on each shift)

- Total of 12 aid positions, 10 full-time and 2 part-time

You can modify the part-time FTE to precisely match the necessary FTE. However, depending upon the actual benefit time of the department, the typical vacancy rate and ongoing education/training time required, the small amount of additional FTE will provide for some contingency (in fact it may not be enough). As the manager, you may want to add 3-4 per diem RN positions to provide additional flexibility and cover the schedule based on seasonal fluctuations with volume and staff vacations. You may consider converting a full-time aid position into two part-time positions, or adding additional per diem positions to enhance flexibility and accommodate the vacancy trends.

One more step: Validate your staffing plan against your budget. To do this you need to fully understand what is in your budget and what should or should not be included (direct care, other fixed time and benefit time).

- Direct care (sometimes called productive time) – the hours invested in direct patient care

- Other fixed (sometimes referred to non-productive time) – management time, administrative time, orientation time, paid time spent in ongoing education, training, committee work. It is time paid that is not providing direct patient care.

- Total paid time – this is the sum of all worked time and benefit time.

Continuing with the example above, let's assume that your department has a direct care worked HPPD of 7.65, meaning that your budget supports 7.65 hours of care for every patient every day. With an average daily census of 20, that is a total of 1,071 hours of care per week. Convert 1,071 into FTEs: 1,071 hours / 40 hours per FTE = 26.78 FTEs. The staffing grid, at the average daily census, requires 25.2 FTEs. (The gird requires 4 RNs and 2 Aids around the clock – 6 associates x 24 hours x 7 days in a week divided by 40 hours per FTE = 25.2 FTEs) The additional 1.58 FTE provides for some flexibility to accommodate the fact that volume dynamic, and staffing fluctuates not only on volume but based on the unique needs the patients require. **What if the direct care worked HPPD was 7.5? How would you change the plan to reduce 21 care hours?** You can also complete this process by starting with your HPPD, identifying the budgeted care hours and building your plan from that point. Either way, it requires deliberate planning. There are a multitude of factors that influence the number and type of positions that you should include in your staffing plan:

- Patient care needs

- Benefit ratio for the variety of roles in the department

- Turnover rate (this will vary by role)

- Typical vacancy rate (this will vary by role)

- Ongoing education and training required (beyond orientation)

- Seasonality of volume

- Seasonality of staff time off

Having the right number of associates doing the right work is important – too many and you risk frustrating your team by reducing their hours and pay or you risk running over budget. Having too few hours means that you run the risk of not meeting the patient needs or overworking your team. It is a balancing act, and if you are not proactively planning and helping your team understand the staffing plan, you will end up constantly chasing staffing issues. Leverage your mentor relationship to work through your staffing plan. Ask your boss for help and clarify your plan before you execute on it.

Interview & Hire the Right Talent

Once you know the number and type of positions you need and where you need them, hire accordingly. Most organizations have a mechanism for managing the number of positions maintained. There may be an approval process required before posting a position. Work with your boss, HR partner and finance partner to gain approval for what is needed. Post available positions, start interviewing and hire the right people to compliment your team. Making the right hiring decisions is an important responsibility and a significant aspect of your role. Check to see if the organization provides an interviewing course for leaders. If offered, add to your list to complete. Some organizations conduct group hiring events, where candidates are hired for the organization and not the individual department. Check with your mentor, boss and HR partner regarding the process for your organization, then leverage the processes and resources available to you.

"Hire integrity, enthusiasm and passion. Develop skill." – Ty Howard, speaker, author, consultant

When you are the one conducting the interview, be deliberate about your process. Create a process that supports conversation and healthy dialogue. It creates a more comfortable interaction, puts the candidate at ease and provides for a less rehearsed and more authentic interaction. The questions you ask and how you ask them are important. Leverage humble inquiry and stay curious about who they are. Listen attentively and avoid making judgments. As the interviewer and hiring manager, you need to assess their skills, abilities and attributes. Use references to help assess competence. Offer up a problem for them to solve and assess their process. You can determine if they have solved it before or how they would go about finding the solution. Evaluate their ability to learn, integrate new information and change. Gauge their versatility and flexibility. Evaluate their skill, ability and attributes through discussion about their work experience, educational background, community involvement and life experiences.

Competence is important, and it is not the only thing that drives a successful selection. Be sure to spend time exploring other attributes. The candidate's character, integrity and heart should match the core values of the organization. **Will they contribute to the team's effectiveness?** Be wary of biases as you make your selections. A homogenous workforce will limit the team's ability. With diversity comes creativity and innovation. **Are they collaborative? Do they appreciate working as a team? How will they advocate for patients? How do they respond when things do not go as planned? Do they value different opinions? Do they demonstrate the articulated values of the organization and department?** Human resource thought-leader, John Sullivan, Professor of Management at San Francisco State University, suggests that, "it's imperative that interviewers get the most critical information out of candidates possible." Sullivan suggests carefully selecting questions and determining the most acceptable answers in advance. He shares guidelines for question development in his *Harvard Business Review* article, "7 Rules for Job Interview Questions That Result in Great Hires."

A strategy that you may want to incorporate into your plan is "peer interviewing." This has gained in popularity and it can be helpful. It does come with its drawbacks, however. Peer interviewing is the process of having current employees talk with a candidate about a job. Candidates have the opportunity to discuss the job with those who are doing the job. Candidates can get a sense of how the team works together. The team becomes more vested in the success of the individuals they select to join their team. Bias can occur as they look for someone who thinks like them. Time necessary to train the peer interviewers as well as time to coordinate the peer interview process may make incorporating peer interviewing into your hiring process too difficult. If you leverage peer interviewing be thoughtful about how you integrate the feedback into your decisions.

Create your interview strategy:

- Be thoughtful, plan to not be interrupted and plan for the conversation

- Build rapport, guide the interaction and facilitate conversation

- Outline the points to be covered and the key messages you need to share; keep this brief so you can listen more than you talk, use a handout if needed (creation of a handout is a great way to get your team involved)

- Identify a few questions that will help you explore required skill, ability and attributes use humble inquiry,

- Sit in silence, give them time to talk and listen, explore more deeply if necessary

- Allow time for the candidate to ask questions

- Wrap up, share next steps and provide a timeline for decision

- Evaluate the responses, make a selection and follow-up

Successful interview and selection practices are ultimately the result of consciously seeking those characteristics that benefit your patient population and the pursuit of excellence you desire.

Making the right hiring decisions will have a significant impact on your team and the patients you serve. Tie your selection criteria and questions to department-relevant standards. To make the best decision, create a deliberate process and stay curious throughout the process, use your authenticity to genuinely share expectations, be resolute in your selections.

Retain Talent

"The simplest way to stop your employees from leaving is to develop a plan to make them stay." – Unknown

According to the 2021 staffing report compiled by the recruitment firm NSI Nursing Solutions, turnover rates continue to increase. In 2020, the turnover rate for staff RNs increased to 18.7%, the highest in a decade. Hospitals' RN vacancy rates average 9.9% – this varies across regions and hospital bed size. Between 2016 and 2020, the average hospital turned over 83% of their RN workforce. In essence, every 6 years, a hospital will have an entirely new RN staff. According to the survey, the cost of turnover for a bedside RN ranges from $28,400 to $51,700. Each percent change in RN turnover will cost/save the average hospital $270,800/yr. Turnover costs organizations more than just financially, quality, safety and service can be jeopardized when vacancies occur. Leaders are forced to focus on staffing and filling gaps rather than other aspects of the business. Overworked staff members are more likely to make mistakes and further contribute to the revolving door phenomenon. A stable workforce enables more consistent care delivery, patient experience and reduced expenses. Retention should be a key focus for all nurse leaders. **What is the turnover in your department? How has turnover changed in the last three to six months? What**

retention strategies are already in place? How are they effective? What else might you do to retain team members?

For years, I heard from human resource colleagues that people do not leave their jobs – they leave their manager. I believe that there are many dynamics that contribute to the turnover that exists among bedside nurses and your leadership is one of these factors that are totally within your control. The role is challenging and as the manager, you can make a huge difference. Leadership style does have an impact on the overall work environment – hence the *READI* attributes. Melina Theodorou shares the study of 1,000 people conducted by Career Addict, an online career resource for millions of readers. In it, she states that 79% of employees would consider quitting because of their boss and 43% would return to their previous role if their boss were replaced.

In a 2017 Forbes article, Victor Lipman stated, "66% of employees say they would likely leave their job if they didn't feel appreciated. This jumps to 76% among millennials." Showing appreciation is fully within your control as the leader. Get creative in how you show appreciation. Make it meaningful. A great resource is *1501 Ways to Reward Employees* by Bob Nelson. This book is full of ideas (1501 ideas) to recognize and celebrate your associates. Show your team how much you appreciate them. Saying "thank you" with specific gratitude goes a long way. *Love 'Em or Lose 'Em,* by Beverly L. Kaye and Sharon Jordan-Evans, is another of my favorite books. It is full of practical tactics to build a culture of engagement to keep employees. However, one of the most important lessons is on the front cover: you have to love 'em if you want to keep 'em. Leading with love means knowing and caring about what inspires and empowers people. It is about caring enough to know what is important so that you can help them succeed in their endeavors. Add this book to your must-have list.

"Appreciation can make a day, even change a life. Your willingness to put it into words is all that is necessary." – Margaret Cousins, writer, educator, women's rights activist

As a leader of people, you must get to know your team. The Nurse Manager span of control can be large and getting to know 100 or more employees can be challenging, even overwhelming.

The payoff however is huge. Get to know them and treat them like the individuals they are – the result of your efforts will reduce turnover and the need to constantly get to know new team members. If you know your people (really know them), then:

- Your communication will be more genuine, intentional and more likely to influence

- You will know their concerns and will be able to help them work through their challenges

- You will know what is important to them and can inspire them to accomplish their goals

- You will have a better understanding of what will keep them

- You will have an engaged team and it will be easier to solve problems together

Simply put, when you really know your team, you're more likely to create an environment for your team to accomplish great things. Following the transition plan outlined in this book will help you create that collaborative supportive work environment. Your *READI* leadership will support the creation of a 'sticky' culture where people do not want to leave.

"People work for money but go the extra mile for recognition, praise and rewards." – Dale Carnegie, professor, author, speaker, pioneer in the field of self-improvement.

Manage Performance

Hiring is critical, and aligning your team for success is even more important. An effective performance management process sets the foundation for aligning individual efforts and organizational goals. Previously I discussed managing your team's talent. It is important to understand that in order to maintain team performance, you must address the performance of individuals. Your role in managing performance is to both help and expect individuals on your team to make the right choice every day. Be resolute in your management, maintain high standards and assume positive intent. Focus on helping your team achieve their goals. Deliberately and authentically address concerns. Assume the positive intent of others. Through respect and humble inquiry, discover what is motivating their choices and establish the steps to encourage, make improvement or re-direction as necessary.

A key aspect of managing performance is recognizing a job well done. Celebrate great performances. Be deliberate, genuine and specific in your praise – it should match the deed. Praise should out number correction by five to one; five positives to every one correction (I have seen this number suggested at 3:1 and as high as 8:1). We, as humans naturally hold on to the negative we hear, it is how our brains are wired. We tend to believe the bad more than the good. This means as a leader you need to be deliberate about recognizing and appreciating the good. Leverage the resources and ideas discussed in the previous discussion about retaining talent and celebrate the good that is happening and the people making it possible. Look for ways to have individuals celebrated at other levels in the organization. Make sure to tell your boss about the good stuff. For your own wellbeing, deliberately spend more time in this headspace, practicing savoring and gratitude. It will give you the energy and courage needed to address performance concerns. Your organization may have formal recognition programs – use them and get creative with your own ideas to celebrate great performance.

When individuals are not meeting expectations, you must take action. Organizations typically have a process to both direct and document your actions. There may be training materials to assist you (if there are training materials take advantage of them). **What is the process at your organization?** When you are addressing a behavior or skill that needs to be corrected, there are deliberate steps to take and conversations to have that may escalate from gentle reminders to termination of employment. Prepare appropriately for these conversations. Use the communication tool shared in chapter six. Each conversation will require you to stay resolute in your purpose, authentic and genuine about your expectations and deliberate about your message. Inquire about what is preventing the individual from meeting the standards expected and empower them to take the actions necessary by sharing the benefits and consequences. Leverage your relationship with your human resource partner, ask your mentor and boss for advice, then proceed with courage. **Are there conversations you are not having? What is holding you back?** Other team members want assurance everyone is held accountable to the standards and the patients in your care deserve the best. Addressing poor performance is essential to the team culture and quality care.

"Nothing will kill a great employee faster than watching you tolerate a bad one" – Perry Belcher, serial entrepreneur

Deliberate and methodical process is required to manage performance and create a high performing team. You need to be intentional not only about your expectations, but how you coach to achieve them. Prioritize your performance management conversations and create a culture where all are expected to grow Evaluate each member of your team and put them into three categories: individuals who consistently meet the standards and are role models to others (these individuals help make the team better), individuals who struggle to meet the standards (these individuals hold the team back) and those in the middle, who show ability but may inconsistently demonstrate skill and behavior. Erie Chapman, in his book *Sacred Work*, describes this as "simple as A B C." He suggests that the goal for us as leaders is to create an "A" style culture and develop "A style" talent. He labels the first group, the consistently high performers, as "A" players. The third group, who hold the team back, is labeled as "C" players, and the middle group is denoted as "B" players. Chapman discusses how both A and C players influence other team members, particularly the B players, who sway their behavior based on who is around. Recognizing the great work of the A players while addressing C players' performance helps to influence B players' choices. Using this tactic to evaluate your team allows you to be more deliberate in your actions and have better communication with each member of your team:

- Meet with the A players and re-recruit them – ask them what would make them stay. Let them know how much you appreciate their contributions. Lyn Ketelson, in the *Nurse Leader Handbook* states, "No doubt acts of everyday heroism take place…many of these accomplishments go unrecognized because others didn't know about them." Be the person to find these heroic moments and make sure others find out about them. Be genuine and authentic in your recognition.

- Meet with the C players and have the appropriate performance management discussions – help them make the right choices. In the end, if they choose not to meet the expectations, you must make the very difficult decision to end their employment. Leverage your human resource partner for help with this. At all times, maintain respect. Be resolute in your purpose and empowered to do what is right.

- Help the B players gain awareness of their inconsistent behavior. Recognize them for a job well done, stay curious about what is driving their inconsistency, reinforce the good and coach for improvement or redirection when necessary.

Additional points:

- Your team will make choices every day, both expect and help them make the right choices. Be clear and specific about expectations. Eliminate ambiguity whenever possible. With clear performance expectations (results, actions and behavior), your team will understand what needs to be done and what it means to be successful on the job.

- Do not let issues linger and do not make knee-jerk decisions. Be deliberate, decisive, and move on with respect, honoring the dignity of others.

- It will be incredibly painful to end an individual's employment, and it will be inevitably better for them when you do. Individuals who are not aligned with your organizational standards will find success when they find alignment elsewhere.

With consistent management of performance – recognizing great performance, coaching for improvement and addressing poor performance, you naturally raise the effectiveness of the team. You will create a culture of accountability and empowerment, where your team will feel more invested in the care delivered. Being invested and feeling a sense of ownership can actually make work more enjoyable for everyone. As the leader, you have the opportunity to make that happen for your team. You have the opportunity to make that happen for your patients. Let your light shine.

"When people feel accountable and included, it is more fun."
– Alan Mulally, aerospace engineer, former CEO of
Ford Motor Company

Performance Appraisals – "Performance management" is a continuous process in which a leader plans, monitors and reviews an employee's work contributions. It occurs through a series of conversations. Conducting performance appraisals is a task that is required by most organizations in order to document individual performance against an established set of expectations. It may or may not be tied to salary adjustments. **What is the performance appraisal process in your organization?**

Below are a few insights for you to be more effective in completing your staff's performance appraisals:

- Start with a clear set of expectations you will evaluate all associates against. If individual goals were established, include these as part of the appraisal.

- Do not surprise anyone. There should not be anything in an appraisal that you have not already shared. This is especially important if the associate is not meeting expectations.

- Be inclusive of the full performance period. Be careful and avoid the recency syndrome where their most recent performance clouds the entire appraisal. Note the performance trend(s) you have observed.

- Be respectful and honest. If there is improvement to be made, note it. Be clear and specific, genuine and authentic. Use examples of actions, behaviors and results. Being falsely positive is hurtful.

- The "written document" is important to validate completion, and the most important part of the appraisal process is the conversation. Be respectful and thoughtful, schedule enough time to discuss the key points you want to share.

"A great review helps your employees identify growth opportunities and potential areas of improvement without damaging employee-manager relations" – Sean Peek, writer, researcher

There are tools to assist you when completing performance appraisals. James Neal's book, *Effective Phrases for Performance Appraisals*, is full of words and phrases to help you acknowledge the contributions and discuss opportunities with professionalism and respect. Dick Grote's book, *How to Be Good at Performance Appraisals*, provides step-by-step advice to successfully complete them. Grote acknowledges that performance appraisals are "demanding and strenuous." It requires unbiased judgment, and that is sometimes difficult. You will need a resolute, deliberate focus to accomplish this. Staying authentic, self-aware, inquisitive and curious will promote productive conversations.

Staff Development and Coaching – Part of any performance management process includes staff development and coaching. Much of what has been covered throughout previous chapters will help you coach and develop your team. Leverage all of your resources and every opportunity to help your team be their best selves. Utilize the opportunities that exist in your organization, such as orientation programs, career ladder programs, other clinical training and online resources. You are not only responsible for monitoring performance, but for making sure that your team has the necessary training to do their jobs correctly. Your goal is to continuously grow your team. As a servant leader you want to grow your team to increase their capacity to deliver care. As a conscious leader you see the development and growth of your team as the best way to serve the most people and achieve the most good.

"Serving people means growing their capacity and implies that everyone can contribute." – Juana Bordas, leadership & diversity activist

Coaching is an important ingredient for development. Coaching is about having quality, developmental conversations to help others grow and succeed. It can occur in casual conversation as well as in more formal settings. Effective coaching is a practiced skill, and like most new skills, it's awkward in the beginning. The term "coaching" has been tossed around throughout my leadership career, and in some instances, it was used as the organizational term for discipline. Although coaching for improvement and redirection can occur, coaching is not telling someone they did something wrong and offering the correct behavior. Coaching is much more than that. It provides guidance but is not discipline. Coaching builds discovery and awareness, empowers choice and leads to change through that learning process. According to Michael Bungay Stainer, author of *The Coaching Habit*, the key to having great coaching conversations is to avoid giving advice or solving problems for others. He stresses that asking a great question, intently listening, then asking the next question will help others discover their own solutions. His book outlines seven questions to guide your conversations. He identifies the attitudes and habits required of managers who desire to motivate and empower their team. I wish I discovered this resource decades ago. It is a must have for your library. The tactics he shared will help you avoid accepting "monkeys" from others.

It feels good to have individuals come to you and ask for advice, to answer their questions, or take control of a situation and rescue them. Be aware of this pattern in your behavior. Consider a new paradigm. Although it may feel good to know the answer, to provide the guidance, and to help, in actuality you are preventing development and damaging the empowerment of your team. It creates a team that is incredibly dependent on you. They will need you in ways that you do not want them to need you. The "do it myself," "rescue," "give advice" habit will prevent you from focusing on the challenges that, as the leader, you should be addressing. Growing your coaching skills will help your team become more self-sufficient, focused and connected to the work. Use the WOOP method discussed earlier to help build your coaching habit.

Provide your team members with tools that will help solve the problems that may arise, and support them without rescuing them. Create the expectation that they are helping each other be their best. Establish standards on how they treat, mentor, teach, interact and engage with one another. Both individual and team development are important to help your staff grow professionally so that they can demonstrate critical clinical leadership at the point of care.

"Good performance accountability is about having a positive conversation between manager and employee. A manager is a coach and communicator, not command and controller." – Dave Ulrich, consultant, writer, professor

Manage The Business

With the six months of experience, you have in the role of Nurse Manager, I am sure you have come to realize just how much there needs to be managed. It is easy to get overwhelmed by the minutia and then fail to see big picture. The previous discussions about how you manage your time, leverage your resources, manage, lead and empower your team all play a role in your ability to balance the big picture and the detail. Managing the business requires the right care delivered at the right time with the right resources. You need to ensure the right resources are available at the right time with the right skill. Your success depends on the ability to accomplish the variety of outcomes that are important to the variety of stakeholders to whom you are responsible. You are managing the business in a complex, matrixed environment. Your role requires you to manage relationships, manage within a budget and deliver on results. To grow your leadership capacity further I will expand on these topics in greater detail.

"Management is, above all, a practice where art, science and craft meet." – Henry Mintzberg, business management professor & author

Leading Within Systems

In chapter three, I discussed the Nurse Manager role, and shared the unique combination of leadership and management required of leaders at the manager level. I suggested that the art was in striking the right balance between leadership and management based on the dynamic forces (inside and outside the organization) that impact the industry, organization and your team.

Create a Matrixed System Map – You are leading within a complex system of systems. I am going to walk you through creating a diagram to illustrate this point.

1. Draw a circle that represents a patient admitted to your department.

2. Around that circle, write each care team discipline that interacts with the patient. Draw a circle around each of them and then draw a line connecting each discipline circle with the patient circle.

3. Around each care team discipline circle, list the regulatory bodies, educational requirements and departments that interact with each of the disciplines to help support patient care. Draw a circle around them and draw a line connecting them to their discipline circle.

4. List the departments that support your team, such as human resources, compliance and finance. Connect them to the nurse circle.

5. List other influencers in the patient's lives, such as their family, church or employer. Draw circles around each and draw a line that connects these circles to the patient.

This complex drawing is where you lead, among several different systems and a complex matrix of relationships. In Peter Drucker's 2002 article in the *Harvard Business Review*, he suggested that the hospital was the most complex human organization ever devised. It is easy to agree with him based on the diagram you just drew. Note – this diagram is from the perspective of just one department's relationship with one patient. **How does your matrixed system map look? Are there areas that create more challenges? Connections that need supported better? Or that could be leveraged better? How are you leading through the challenges?**

An understanding of "systems thinking" and "complexity theory" is important as you learn more about your responsibilities and how to effectively lead in your role. Complex, adaptive systems have complex behaviors. Each system is seeking to accomplish their own responsibilities and goals. "Systems thinking" is based on the principle that the unique components of the system can best be understood in the context of the relationships with each other and other systems. According to Tim Sullivan, the whole of the system is greater than the sum of its parts, and it is hard to understand complex adaptive systems by looking at individual components. Thinking back to my nursing theory courses, Sr. Callista Roy, Betty Neuman and Martha Rogers each described nursing within complex systems and the interdependencies of the elements. Embracing complexity theory is challenging. We strive for cause and effect, and we look for "simple". Doing so can significantly limit our understanding and inhibit our ability to make significant and sustainable improvements.

"Chaos was the law of nature; Order is the dream of man" – Henry Adams, historian, US ambassador

Healthcare delivery is a dynamic business because of its complex adaptive system. Your role as leader can seem chaotic as the individuals and groups of the system interact. You will be faced with problems needing to be addressed within the chaos. Nurses, Mary W. Chaffee, and Margaret M. McNeill suggest that managers who accept that the healthcare industry, the healthcare system and the profession of nursing are complex adaptive systems will be able to create new levers for positive movement in their organizations. Your desire will be to find simplicity in solutions. However, you cannot ignore the complexity of the interacting variables within the system. Changing one part of a system impacts other parts of the system. One of the greatest statistical minds of the 20th century, George E. P. Box, once said, "The only way to know how a complex system will behave after you modify it – is to modify it and see how it behaves." When you alter one aspect of your department processes, it will have an impact on other parts of the organization. You may not always be able to predict the impact. The same is true for other departments that make changes. Assume positive intent if tension occurs. Growing your understanding about the dynamic nature of the system(s) you are engaged in and helping your team understand will further empower you and your team to engage productively and address conflicts that may rise. Be mindful of the complex system you are working within, don't let the complexity prevent you from taking steps, even small steps to improve it. Learn from the results you experience.

The most important thing you can do is to maintain awareness. Consider the diagram I had you draw earlier. It is about collaboration, while also highlighting how embracing diverse opinions and creativity is important to find simplicity within a complex network. Appreciate the multitude of interdependencies so you can be more deliberate in your actions. Early in your onboarding, I suggested that you list all of the key stakeholders you need to invest in growing relationships. I shared a strategy with you to foster strong collaborative working connections. These relationships are critical as you lead within the complex system. These relationships will not only bridge gaps to bring teams together, but they will also be used to gain insight, challenge your opinions and enable you to make even better improvements. **How are you growing your relationships so you can grow your influence? How are you investing in your network?**

"Everyone in a complex system has a slightly different interpretation. The more interpretations we gather, the easier it becomes to gain a sense of the whole." – Margaret Wheatley, author, teacher, speaker, & management consultant

Manage Your Relationships

Dr. Rex Rogers discusses the need for interaction, that we need social interaction for our wellbeing and for achievement. He shares, "People only go it alone when pride, greed, or hurt displaces common sense and experience. Even the Lone Ranger didn't go it alone." In their book *Advancing Relationship-Based Cultures,* Mary Koloroutis and David Abelson state, "Healthy relationships are formed when people consistently attune to one another, wonder with and about one another, follow cues provided by one another and hold one another with respect and dignity." The people around you are critical to your success. I cannot stress this point enough. Invest the time in people. Executive coach Joel Garfinkle shares the following steps to build positive relationships:

- Share more of yourself at meetings

- Speak positively about the people you work with, including your boss

- Improve interpersonal skills by supporting other people's work

- Ask others to become involved in your projects and activities

- Write "thank you" notes

- Initiate conversation by asking questions

- Initiate repeated interactions and communications

- Participate in activities with others that do not involve work

- Share information

- Introduce yourself at social work events

I will add a few more:

- Use humble inquiry when asking about them or their work and listen attentively

- Offer and accept help

- Manage your boundaries

- Be positive, while focusing on the possibilities, avoid scarcity thinking

- Do what you said you would do

- Assume positive intent and lean into resolving conflict

Use your *READI* leadership to support your relationships. Stay resolute in your pursuit to build strong, collaborative ties. Empower them and share authentically as you impart information. Stay deliberate in your focus on them and how you can better work together. Keep an inquiring spirit, stay curious about who they are and what you can learn. **How are you doing while navigating through your relationship heat map? What discoveries are you making? Who may need to be added?**

"Be more concerned about making others feel good about themselves than you are in making them feel good about you." – John Maxwell, leadership author, coach & speaker

Manage Conflict

Conflict is a part of human nature. It is a normal part of a team's functioning. It will influence your relationships. It is important for you, as a leader, to navigate it, manage it and maintain relationships through it. Throughout my career, I have heard many leaders discuss how they wished the organization's leaders had more skills with which to "manage conflict." This is a skill like so many others, needs to be practiced. You can read about it, yes, and in the end, you must have the courage to lean in and accept that it is natural. Try not to take issues personally and help your team and peers resolve conflict when it arises. It is easy to get a bit anxious when conflict does arise. It is important to also understand that conflict can be productive. Conflict can lead to innovation and enhanced problem solving when dissenting opinions are heard. Creativity is stimulated. When conflict is appropriately managed, the work environment is healthier, more collaborative and knowledgeable.

For nearly half a century, Kenneth Thomas and Ralph Kilmann's conflict assessment model has been implemented to help leaders, at all levels, enhance their skills as they lead through conflict. The Thomas-Kilmann Conflict Mode Instrument (TKI) provides insight into how different conflict styles affect personal and group dynamics. It is based on the assumption that we all "default" to a particular style. As with most leadership skills, one style is not the best for all situations. Each of the styles described in the TKI has their appropriateness, benefits and drawbacks.

Self-awareness, again, is an important first step in growing your skill managing conflict. The TKI model is an assessment that describes your tendencies when faced with conflict. TKI identifies two dimensions when choosing a course of action in a conflict situation: assertiveness and cooperativeness. Both are on a continuum determined by our assertiveness (the degree we attempt to satisfy our own concerns) and our cooperativeness (the degree we attempt to satisfy the concerns of others). According to Thomas and Kilmann's conflict instrument, there are 5 key styles to managing conflict:

- Competing (assertive, non-cooperative) – using authority or power to satisfy your own concerns; standing up for your rights, defending a position you believe is correct and wanting to win.

- Accommodating (unassertive, cooperative) – focus on satisfying the other's concern while neglecting your own; accommodating is the opposite of competing; selfless generosity or charity and obeying another's authority even when you would prefer not to, or yielding to another's opinion.

- Avoiding (unassertive, uncooperative) – ignoring the conflict or not taking any action to resolve it; sidestepping an issue, postponing until a "better" time or withdrawing from a threatening situation.

- Compromising (intermediate degree of assertiveness and cooperativeness) – attempting to resolve the conflict by finding solutions that are partially satisfactory to both but completely satisfactory to neither; splitting the difference, exchanging concessions or seeking a quick middle-ground position.

- Collaborating (both cooperative and assertive) – cooperating to understand each other's concerns in an effort to find a mutually satisfying solution; exploring a disagreement to learn from each other's insights; exploring options to address both concerns or confronting to find a creative solution mutually supportive resolution.

"The Law of Win/Win says, 'Let's not do it your way or my way; let's do it the best way." – Greg Anderson, musician & composer

Typically, the "collaboration" style is most effective in interactions with your colleagues. Building trusting relationships will require a focus on cooperation without abdicating your own or your department's needs. You will want to grow the skills to professionally engage in conflict, build mutual understanding and find win-win solutions. The collaboration style is more likely to lead to learning, consensus, trust and innovation. Although this style may be most useful to foster strong working relationships and help your team grow, there is no style that is right every time. All five styles are useful depending on the situation, and each represents a set of useful social skills. There will be times when you must use the "competing" style to enforce a policy or protocol that is not up for debate. There are times when "accommodating" is the most effective style because you want to preserve harmony or minimize disruption. You may choose accommodating when you accept a rule or policy you do not like, yet, do not wish to invest energy in changing. You may choose the compromise style when time does not offer a collaborative solution or when the solutions are in opposition – you may "split the difference" and compromise. And there will be times when you choose the avoiding style, when other issues take priority, someone else is better able to resolve the issue more effectively or the issue is peripheral to your responsibilities. The conflict behavior you use is the result of your personal predispositions, versatility and the requirements of the unique situation. Take steps to be fully aware and deliberate in your choice of style. Match the style to the situation.

Let's discuss building the collaboration style for conflict resolution a bit further. I have found two resources to be helpful as developing conflict management skill. The first is *Crucial Conversations*, a framework for engaging in challenging conversations. The second is *The 15 Commitments of Conscious Leadership*, a process where you develop "radical" self-awareness and "radical" responsibility for your own reality. Both are key ingredients to healthy relationships and are essential for healthy conflict in the people-based world in which you lead and manage.

Resolving conflict through collaboration requires mutual respect and understanding. It requires courage and conversation. You need courage to engage in conversations that are high stakes, where our (and others) approval, security, or control may be at stake. This is sensitive territory and should be navigated thoughtfully. *Crucial Conversations* by Kerry Patterson, Joseph Grenny, Ron McMillan and Al Switzer helped me develop the courage and skill to engage in difficult conversations, while assisting me to address conflict in a healthier way. *Crucial Conversations* helped me to understand that when I was stuck in a conflict, or just stuck, simply having a conversation would get me unstuck, or at least get me into problem-solving again. The authors suggest, "When it comes to risky, controversial and emotional conversations, skilled people find a way to get all relevant information (from themselves and others) out in the open." I agree that when you can reach that point of a true collaborative conversation, you will achieve a breakthrough. Through the *Crucial Conversations* course, I learned to be more effective while engaging in challenging conversations. Leaning into these conversations actually helped me to prevent conflict. This skill of healthy dialogue, the authors refer to as the critical "one thing" to drive success. *Crucial Conversations* provides a framework to guide you through conversations that keep the dialogue open so you can eventually move into action. It starts with honoring your own worth, while honoring the worth of others. To engage you must know yourself, know what you really want, and create phycological safety for all participants. You must share, yet be willing to challenge your own opinions, and attentively hear the opinions of others. *Crucial Confrontations* by the same authors provides further guidance as you engage in even more challenging conversations. I recommend both as "must-haves" for your library.

> *"The void created by the failure to communicate is soon filled with poison, drivel and misrepresentation."* – Cyril Northcote Parkinson, British naval historian, author

To be successful in challenging conversations self-awareness is critical. Through conscious leadership we become radically self-aware enabling us to take full responsibility for our thoughts, behaviors and decisions. In his article, *5 Keys to Being Conscious in Conflict*, Jim Dethmer offers five "keys" to help transformational leaders navigate conflict to help themselves and their teams find win/win solutions, while rising to new levels of effectiveness:

- Hold your story lightly and encourage others to do the same. We make sense out of facts that we see by interpreting these facts into a story. That story created is our opinion. We all have them, and our opinion is one of many about the same facts. Be honest about your own story and learn as much as you can about the story others have. Dethmer suggests that destructive leadership happens when there is a fight to be right about our own story, "It is needing to be seen by everyone as being right that causes dysfunctional conflict."

- Listen deeply from the head, heart and gut. According to Dethmer, "The environment for all unhealthy conflict is non-listening." He goes on to say, "It is impossible to have destructive conflict if all parties deeply listen to one another." Humble inquiry and maintaining a curious, learning spirit will help you manage conflict.

- Face what you most want to avoid facing. Conflict arises when we ignore or fail addressing a core issue. Dethmer shares that great leaders face their deepest issues "squarely, courageously and humbly."

- Commit to "win for all" solutions. In other words, try for a win/win. Focus on opportunity, not scarcity. When we focus on what we can all gain versus what we can individually lose, we will achieve resolution.

- Do not take the conflict seriously. This seems contradictory – if it is worth having a disagreement over, should it not be taken seriously? Once we believe our basic wants are threatened, we go into autonomic fight, flight, freeze or faint mode. None of these are helpful in the typical social or work conflicts that exist in our lives today. Stay in full consciousness and prevent the autonomic response. According to Dethmer, "Great leaders learn that from a distance nothing is serious." This practice will help you objectively look at the situation, regulate yourself and resolve the conflict in a healthy way.

"A good manager doesn't try to eliminate conflict; he tries to keep it from wasting the energies of his people." – Robert Townsend, business executive & author

When you can look at conflict as an opportunity to learn, grow and develop, you see that it is a productive experience. Your *READI* leadership will enable you to manage conflict. Be resolute and true to your purpose. Hold tightly to your purpose and loosely to your opinions as you engage in conversations. Be resolute in learning what you can learn and understand the best solution, not just your solution. You are empowered, take responsibility to do what is right in the right way and be respectful to others. Own your part of the conflict and apologize if you need to. Help others to take their own responsibility. Be authentic and self-aware. Pay attention to your emotions, stories, feelings and desires. Your vulnerability will help to create psychological safety for others. Be deliberate in your actions and prepare for challenging conversations. Be intentional about your tone of voice and the words you choose. Be inquisitive, stay curious about what you can learn and how you can foster a stronger relationship as you invest in the dialogue. **Are you avoiding conflict? How may you foster a deeper connection if you work through conflict that may exist? What do you need to do to engage in conflict more effectively?**

Manage the Financials

A key competency for you to develop is business acumen. Based on my experience, this is the area that I see many first-time leaders struggle, particularly those leaders who come from clinical backgrounds. Most nurses that I talk to have limited knowledge about the budgets in their organizations and oftentimes, they do not care to learn. The general attitude is that the "finances" are the responsibility of the administrators, not the caregivers. This is flawed thinking. The growing pressures on the healthcare industry to control the rapidly escalating expense of healthcare will require nurses at all levels to deepen their understanding of the business. Our patients and communities need us, as caregivers, to be aware of the connection between how we use resources and the cost of care delivery. **What does this mean for you as a leader?** The CEO of your company needs you to understand how your department contributes to the bottom-line of the organization. Your team needs you to advocate for the resources needed and ensure their security by being fiscally responsible. As the manager, you need to grow your own competency. You need to learn, build, monitor and explain an operating budget. You need to develop proposals for capital investments that need to be made. In addition, you need to be an interpreter and teacher. You need to advocate for the needs of your department and the patients you serve. You need to teach others what is required for care delivery and teach your team to accept responsibility for the resources (stuff and time) they use.

I do want to share a few basic concepts to help you grow your competence in terms of healthcare finances. I encourage you to leverage your boss and mentor relationships as you navigate the specific processes at your organization. As you were identifying key stakeholders, I encouraged you to identify a partner in the finance department. Leverage this relationship as well. Absorb what you can and stay inquisitive to continue learning. Nurses are trained from a scientific background. We studied mathematics to ensure we could calculate medication doses. Do not let the language of finance intimidate you. Absorb and learn what you can, while asking questions. You will quickly grasp the concepts. Understanding the business operations will enhance your credibility as a leader when you are talking to senior leaders. At this point in your first year, you have most likely completed variance reports, depending on your department's financial metrics. You will need to prepare an annual budget for the next fiscal year and determine any capital investments required. Experience is a great teacher so be sure to prioritize this learning in the context of everything on your list.

Capital verses Operating – Capital expenses are large investments in fixed assets, such as equipment or facilities. Organizations establish a threshold expense per item to be considered capital. For example, as a manager, I needed to purchase blood pressure cuffs and a new lift chair. The blood pressure cuffs were less than the threshold limit, and the lift chair was more than the operating expense limit. Therefore, I sent through the purchase request for the blood pressure cuffs and I expensed them to the minor equipment account of my operating budget. I needed to go through the capital request process for the lift chair. **What is the operating expense limit in your organization?** Capital investments are typically assessed once a year. Requests are accepted and often prioritized based on the return on investment (ROI). Depending on the request, you may need to complete an ROI, in which you justify the expense by identifying reduced expenses or enhanced revenue to support the purchase price. Requests are granted based on the capital funds available in the given timeframe. **What have you learned about the capital process at your organization? What is the capital request timeline in your organization? What, if any, capital requests may your department require?**

Your operating budget is managed monthly, biweekly or even daily in some aspects. Your operating budget includes your department's labor expense, supplies and minor equipment. It also includes the revenue that is generated from your department. During fiscal planning cycles, the volumes, revenue and expenses are determined and your responsibility is to manage these metrics, understand the drivers of each and be able to explain variances if they occur. Most organizations operate on an annual budget. The fiscal year may be managed according to a calendar year, July through June, or October through September. Regardless of the fiscal year, you will be responsible for developing an annual operating budget for your department. **What is the timeline at your organization to develop the operating budget? How is your operating budget established?** Even if the organization does not have a robust budget cycle, you will be responsible for understanding your financial operations and managing productivity. Let's dig into some components of the operating budget a bit further.

Revenue – For most nursing departments, revenue is driven by volume. On inpatient units, it is typically determined based on a room rate. In outpatient areas, revenue may be degenerated by procedures, visits or by time spent in the department. **What are the revenue drivers in your department?** It is most common for volume to drive the charges that come from your department. **What is the expected volume in your department? What is the actual volume?** The gross charges do not necessarily equal the actual reimbursement or revenue received. Your organizations' contractual arrangements with the payers will determine revenue. Revenue may be based on a total diagnostic group (DRG) or by volume. This may differ among payers, and some may pay only 30-40 cents for every dollar charged. Depending on how the organization is paid, whether by total care contracts or by volume, it will drive incentives for how revenue is managed and how volume is tracked. More and more payers are moving toward an overall stay payment structure, meaning, for specific diseases, there is a predetermined agreed upon payment. The healthcare industry is moving away from a "pay for volume" to a "pay for value" concept. For you, this means managing length of stay and resources utilized. Every day, an inpatient stay in the hospital is an additional expense. Every additional supply that is used for a procedure is an added expense. **Where is your organization in the journey to value?**

You have an incredible opportunity to demonstrate the value of nursing by creating robust processes that coordinate care to meet patient needs while only using the resources necessary for that patient. In your role as Nurse Manager, you have an incredible opportunity to impact revenue from the value perspective. The work you do leading your team to provide an exceptional experience has significant bearing on revenue. When you are successful in preventing serious safety events, you reduce harm to the patient and financial penalties to the organization. When you follow identified best practices, you support the organizations' ability to receive incentives for care delivered. By following exceptional service standards, where patients feel "cared for" "cared about" and "included," they are more likely to choose your organization when they need care in the future. Do not underestimate the impact of your leadership. **How do the outcomes from your department impact the organizations pay for performance revenue?**

Expense – You will see a variety of expenses on your expense reports, including things like labor, supplies, equipment, facility charges (for maintenance and repair) etc. Supplies and labor are typically the major expense drivers for Nurse Managers. You and your team have direct control over the labor that is utilized and the supplies that are taken into patient rooms. For most organizations, nursing labor is a significant part of the labor pool and overall expenses. This puts significant pressure on nurse leaders to ensure appropriate staffing and maintain productivity. In organizations that I have been a part of, the overall labor expense was more than 50% of the overall expenses. In those organizations, the nursing workforce made up 25-30% of the overall workforce. The nursing community, in any organization, has a huge responsibility to be good stewards of the resources and to help manage expenses. Nurse leaders cannot do this without the support of their teams. Hence the need to grow the business acumen competency among nurses at all levels. **What percentage of the organization's expenses are labor expenses? What percentage of your monthly expenses are labor expenses? Supply expenses?**

Manage Productivity – The best way to manage expenses while ensuring appropriate resources to deliver patient care is by managing productivity. Productivity measures outputs over inputs – the investments made to deliver care divided by the volume of patients to care for. The number of nursing staff required and the supplies utilized is dependent on the number (and type) of patients served. These expenses vary. You should evaluate your labor and supply expense based on a unit of service, not a flat, monthly allowance. When you have more patients, you use more supplies and have more staff providing care. The inverse is also true. Looking at hours, labor expenses and supply use per unit of service allows you to manage expenses more precisely.

Let's walk through a labor productivity scenario: You are the manager of a 24-bed inpatient unit and room charges are generated at midnight every night. Your staffing plan is based on 12-hour shifts and nurse staffing is built on a 1:5 nurse to patient ratio. Your paid HPPD is 9.25. In addition to you as the manager you have an educator who works 20 hours a week dedicated to meeting educational requirements in the department. This particular pay period you had two individuals on orientation. The volumes on your unit and the staffing over a two-week time frame looked like this:

Day	7am-7pm	7pm-7am	Midnight census
Sunday	3 RNs 1 aid (+ 1 hr. extra time)	3 RNs (+ 1 hr. extra time)	12
Monday	5 RNs 2 aids (+ 2 hrs extra time)	5 RNs, 1 aid (+ 1 hr. extra time)	22
Tuesday	5 RNs 2 aids (+ 1 hr. extra time)	5 RNs, 2 aids (+ 1 hr. extra time)	21
Wednesday	5 RNs, 2 aids	4 RNs, 2 aids (+ 1 hr. extra time)	20
Thursday	5 RNS, 2 aids (+ 2 hrs extra time)	5 RNs, 2 aids (+ 2 hrs extra time)	24
Friday	5 RNs, 2 aids (+ 1 hr. extra time)	4RNs, 2 aids (+ 1 hr. extra time)	19
Saturday	4RNs, 2 aids (+ 1 hr. extra time)	4RNs, 1 aid (+ 1 hr. extra time)	17
Sunday	4RNs, 2 aids (+ 1 hr. extra time)	3 RNs, 1 aid	14
Monday	5 RNs, 2 aids	4RNs, 2 aids	20
Tuesday	5 RNs, 2 aids (+2 hrs extra time)	5 RNs, 2 aids (+2 hrs extra time)	23
Wednesday	5 RNs, 2 aids (+ 1 hr. extra time)	5 RNs, 2 aids (+ 2 hr. extra time)	22
Thursday	5 RNs, 2 aids	4RNs, 2 aids	19
Friday	5 RNs, 2 aids (+ 1 hr. extra time)	4RNs, 2 aids (+ 1 hr. extra time)	20
Saturday	4 RNs, 2 aids	4RNs, 1 aid	16
	94 individual shifts x 12 hours each + 12 hrs = 1,140 hours	81 individual shifts x 12 hours each +13 hrs = 985 hours	269 total patient days

The average daily census was 19.2 patients/day (269 total patient days/14 days = 19.2)

The average skill mix used was 70.8% RN (124 RN shifts/175 total shifts = 70.8). Skill mix can also be calculated on total hours of RN worked divided by total hours.

In this example, your direct care hours-per-patient (HPPD) day is 7.91. Total of 2,125 hours divided by 269 patient days.

Add the fixed time that was accrued:

- Your leadership hours (40 hours/week = 80 hours)

- 2 staff members on orientation each for 40 hours/week (160 hours).

- Educator (20 hours/week - 40 hours).

These additional hours make your worked HPPD 8.94. (2,125 direct care hours + 280 additional worked hours = 2405 total worked hours. 2405 hours/269 patient days = 8.94)

Consider the paid time off that your team took. For the sake of this example consider, you have one individual who took a week of vacation pay (36 hours), one individual who called in sick (12 hours) and another individual who is off on maternity leave (36 hours/week - 72 hours). Your paid HPPD is 9.39. (2405 total worked hours + 120 additional paid hours = 2,525 total paid hours. 2,525 paid hours/269 patient days = 9.39)

The budgeted HPPD is 9.25; your department ran 37 hours over for this two-week period. (9.25 HPPD x 269 patient days = 2,488 hours. 2,525 total hours paid – 2,488 hours allotted = 37 hours. You want to work to understand these 37 hours. Questions you may ask:

- **Was the fixed time used consistent with the budget plan?**

- **Was the paid time used consistent with the budget plan?**

- **What orientation time is built into the budget plan?**

- **Did the volume have a positive or negative impact on the fixed/paid HPPD?**

- **What was the staff's excess extra time during this period?**

- **Was the staffing flexed to the volume appropriately?**

"Productivity is never an accident. It is the result of commitment to excellence, intelligent planning and focused effort." – Paul J Meyer, self-improvement business owner, author & educator

When you understand the building blocks to managing productivity, you can more easily explain variances and manage expenses. Here are a couple of points that I want to share regarding the example:

- The extra time (which is common) can add up. "Extra time" is the time beyond the scheduled shift. For example, a nurse expected to work a 12-hour shift stays beyond the end of the shift to complete a few tasks, she works 12.5 hours instead, equaling 0.5 hours of extra time. In the two-week scenario, the department experienced 25 hours of extra time. That is, essentially, an additional part-time associate that was used. There were 175 individual shifts, assuming each staff member worked a full 12-hour shift. That means, on average, each associate only clocked out 8-9 minutes late each shift.

Managing this is sensitive. To the individual, you are talking about 8-9 minutes but for the department, it is a significant amount of time. As you are leading to manage productivity, work with your teams. Support their wellbeing and activities that will help them get their work completed so they can get lunch breaks and leave on time. **How often are your team members working beyond their shift? How often do they miss lunch? What trends do you see? What KPIs might you consider monitoring?**

- In the example, your time as the leader, is considered fixed time. It is time paid regardless of the volumes. In the example, this time equated to just 1.04 of the worked HPPD. The average census over the two weeks was 19 patients/day. Consider that the department volumes would have an average of 21 patients a day. The fixed hours would have equated to 0.95 HPPD. If the average daily census was 17 patients per day, the fixed hours would equate to 1.18 HPPD. This may seem trivial, yet over the course of the year, fixed time can have a significant impact on your productivity. **How does fixed time in your department impact your HPPD?**

- A similar phenomenon occurs with the paid not-worked time. Paid not-worked time divided over a smaller number of patients will inflate your HPPD. Paid time divided among more patients will make your HPPD look more efficient.

- The targeted nurse to patient ratio was 1:5 in this department. If you evaluate the staffing based on the midnight census, you may say that the department was overstaffed. You need to take into consideration the fluctuations in volume that occur over the course of the day. When creating a staffing plan and preparing a budget, be sure to consider the routine variations in volume that your department experiences. For example: if the annual volume equated to an average of 20 patients a day, you may consider staffing the day shift for 22 patients a day. In order to make that call, you need to know your department. Collect the information to be as prepared as you can. **How does patient volume fluctuate in your department? What trends do you see? How do these fluctuations impact your department HPPD? How might you monitor this using a daily KPI?**

- Staff planning and scheduling are vital ingredients to appropriately managing productivity. Although the example did not discuss salary dollars, productivity can also be shared in salary dollars per patient day. Overtime hours, temporary agency staffing and other premium pay hours can significantly impact your overall salary cost. It is important to pay attention to salary dollars and hours. Both contribute to expense management. Both also contribute to the care that is delivered and the pateints' experience of that care.

- Some organizations monitor FTEs per adjusted occupied bed (AOB). This is a sophisticated calculation that includes revenue generated, department FTEs and an allocation of overhead labor. **What is the FTE per AOB in your department? How does your organization use FTE per AOB to manage the business?**

- When discussing productivity, be clear about what is included and not included. Make sure you are on the same page with your boss, the finance representative or whomever you are speaking with. Misunderstanding can easily happen – before answering a question or inquiry, make sure you understand the question and the data being referenced.

Consider the scenario and think about your own department. What is your direct care, worked and paid HPPD? What is your budgeted average daily census? How much extra time does your department use every pay period? What is your salary per patient day? What is your salary per patient discharge? How much orientation time is your department paying? What is the expected FTE per occupied bed? Is your department appropriately flexing to the volume? Are your metrics meeting budget? Do you know why or why not? Are there KPIs you could be monitoring with your team? Once you understand the building blocks, you can make sense out of so much. There are many ways to break down the hours and tighten labor expenses when you understand the full breadth of the calculations.

As you gain understanding of the financial impact from your decisions, you will gain influence with your boss and other senior leaders. You are more likely to get resources based on sound explanations. With knowledge comes awareness of how you can support the organizations financial stability. You will think like an owner. As you learn more, engage your team. Help them connect their work with the expenses incurred and with their responsibility to the communities you serve. Help them understand the impact that they make to the bottom line through quality care and an exceptional experience. Solicit their help in finding the right solutions, while maintaining the right number of hands taking care of the patients. Ask for their help collecting the data necessary to advocate for what is needed. Teach them so they can become better stewards themselves. Leverage your READI leadership.

Stay resolute to the purpose of delivering excellent care. You are empowered to make the right decisions. Be authentic, tell your story utilizing the data and make others see what you see. Be deliberate in your analysis and decision-making. Stay inquisitive, use humble inquiry, gain insights and share your learning.

Drive Results

"Some people want it to happen, some wish it would happen, others make it happen." – Michael Jordan, professional athlete

Your success depends on your ability to make "it" happen. Your job is to achieve results – safety, quality service, employee engagement and financial results. You are expected to accomplish improvements in care delivery and service while enhancing the work environment and improving employee engagement. You and your team will be expected to deliver exceptional care, meeting regulatory requirements while managing expenses. You will need to support the organizations' efforts for growth and other initiatives. During your first 60 and 90 days, you established goals and created action plans. I encouraged you to leverage your resources, use rapid cycle improvement and visual management to learn and design new processes. I shared concepts to help you align your team, inspire innovation and work through change. After your first three months in the role, I encouraged you to spend time reflecting on your leadership and make adjustments to become more effective. All of these discussions will help you drive toward results. Author Tony Robbins said, "Where focus goes, energy flows." Your consistent leadership, your championing of the goals and your focus will enable achievement. Football great, Vince Lombardi, said, "Leaders are made, they are not born. They are made by hard effort, which is the price which all of us must pay to achieve any goal that is worthwhile."

Stay *resolute* in your purpose, focused on the future you want to realize, persistent and determined to create a better reality. Inspire a shared vision and build excitement about what can be accomplished.

"People respond well to those that are sure of what they want." – Anna Wintour, longtime editor in chief of American Vogue magazine

You are *empowered* – accept authority for which the organization has entrusted you with managing. Build commitment among your team to consistently deliver excellent patient care. Leverage the intellectual horsepower of your team as you empower them to achieve the results they never thought possible.

"It is surprising how much you can accomplish if you don't care who gets the credit." – Abraham Lincoln, US president

Be *authentic*. Wholeheartedly share your desires. Demonstrate empathy, understanding and care while pursuing your goals. Grow your self-awareness, foster strong, collaborative and trusting relationships to enhance your sphere of influence. Take the work you do, not yourself, seriously.

"A genuine leader is not a searcher for consensus but a molder of consensus." – Martin Luther King Jr, minister & civil rights activist

Take *deliberate* action. Role model your expectations. Encourage others to be intentional in their behavior, consistently following standards. Enable others to act by removing obstacles. Use careful and thoughtful planning. Build reliable processes to accomplish outcomes.

"If you are going to achieve excellence in big things, you develop the habit in little matters. Excellence is not an exception; it is a prevailing attitude." – Colin Powell, politician, diplomat and retired four-star general

Stay *inquisitive* and humble enough to ask the right questions in search of deeper meaning. Find the learning in failures to create new possibilities. Maintain an open mind while staying curious and committed to learning. Foster learning among your team and search for alternative perspectives and differing opinions.

"We keep moving forward, opening new doors, and doing new things, because we're curious and curiosity keeps leading us down new paths." – Walt Disney, animator, writer, actor producer

Your *READI* leadership will help you achieve results to make an impact. In the words of The Chief Operating Officer of Facebook, Sheryl Sandberg, "Leadership is about making others better as a result of your presence and making sure that impact lasts in your absence."

12 Months: Grow Your Leadership

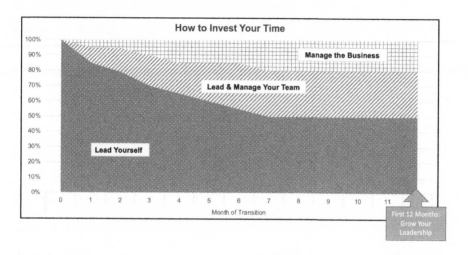

Actions to take:

✓ Manage your calendar

  – Further deploy your visibility plan

  – Continue to progress through your relationship heat map

  – Continue to check off the processes you are learning and doing independently

  – Schedule a quarterly uninterrupted day for reflection and planning

✓ Leverage your mentor relationship as you continue to develop

✓ Integrate what you are learning to change your behavior where appropriate

✓ Identify the formal development opportunities available to you

✓ Review the AONL Nurse Manager Competencies and consider a timeline for certification in the practice of nursing leadership

✓ Practice routine reflection

✓ Evaluate how you are spending your time

✓ Build habits to improve your energy

✓ Leverage W.O.O.P. to build new habits

✓ Build a staffing plan to support your department operations

✓ Create your hiring plan

✓ Reinforce your visibility plan to ensure regular, intentional conversations with all of your people

✓ Evaluate your team's individual performances and provide the right coaching or discipline to ensure performance meets standards

✓ Build a coaching habit

✓ Avoid reacting and "just" answering questions when your team approaches you with a problem – consider asking a question and facilitating their own discovery

✓ Avoid accepting responsibility for what others should keep

✓ Create a Matrixed System Map, evaluate your interdependencies and your relationships

✓ Reflect on your own conflict style

✓ Follow the financial calendar, create your capital requests, operating budget and negotiate for the resources you need to deliver care and manage productivity

✓ Leverage PDSA, KPIs, Visual Management and other tools to drive results

Tools shared:

✓ Savoring

✓ Gratitude

✓ Random Acts of Kindness

✓ W.O.O.P

✓ ABC for Performance Management

✓ Matrix System Map

✓ Steps to grow positive relationships

✓ Staffing grid

✓ TKI

Must haves for your library:

✓ *Love'em or Lose'em* by Beverly L. Kaye and Sharon Jordan-Evans – it is full of strategies to foster retention and engagement.

✓ *The Coaching Habit: Say Less, Ask More & Change the Way You Lead Forever* by Michael Bungay Stainer – will help you become more effective in facilitating problem solving among your team and will save you time.

✓ *Crucial Conversations: Tools for Talking When the Stakes are High* and *Crucial Confrontations: Tools for Resolving Broken Promises, Violated Expectations and Bad Behavior* by Kerry Patterson, Joseph Grenny, Ron McMillan and Al Switzer – both will help you grow your relationships and manage conflict in a healthy way, even when the stakes are high.

Quick tip hints for success:

✓ Schedule quarterly uninterrupted time to reflect and plan – a regular practice of getting away and strategizing will give you renewed energy, help you stay proactive and deliberate versus being reactive and ineffective.

✓ Go to https://conscious.is/,click on the resources page and review the video clips to reinforce your development as a conscious leader with radical self-awareness and radical responsibility.

✓ When you facilitate performance appraisals, pay attention to your consistency in applying standards. Keep your "yardstick" consistent as you measure individual performance and offer feedback.

✓ Work your staffing plan from the bottom up and the top down. Ensure that you can manage the productivity of the unit at the most common census levels and the typical daily fluctuations. ensure that you have the right number of resources available to care for the patients in your care. Proactively fill positions when you know someone is leaving. Commit to helping your team make sound staffing decisions.

✓ Stay *READI* and lead to share your own light and inspire the light in others.

The End – Just the Beginning

"The leader is the person who brings a little magic to the moment." – Denise Morrison, businesswoman, former CEO, Campbell Soup

The conclusion of your first twelve months marks the beginning of your future. You have a full year under your belt, and you have navigated through numerous "firsts." Patti Labelle said," Every exit is an entrance to someplace." You are now entering a new phase in your development as a Nurse Manager and leader. Looking back at your first year, I wish you incredible satisfaction. **When you look back and see the person you were, what do you notice? How has your leadership evolved?** This first year is the foundation for your leadership career – to grow your influence in service to others, model the way, inspire a shared vision and challenge processes to make them better, enable others to act and encourage hearts. My hope is that you continue to grow your self-awareness, build strong, healthy communities, and collaborative teams focused on achieving great things, and you realize your influence and act with courage to tackle the challenges you face. The Nurse Manager Role is critical for the success of the healthcare industry. Leading at the point of care requires *resolute, empowered, authentic, deliberate* and *inquisitive* leadership.

READI leadership is a balance of attributes that exhibit strength and vulnerability, determination and flexibility, risk taking and methodical planning, humbleness and confidence, courage, genuineness, self-awareness, curiosity and agility. *READI* leadership fosters engagement while managing accountability, enables achievement through team ownership, and supports innovation and creativity while managing process. It strives for excellence with a relentless pursuit of compassionate, safe, quality care delivery. Your *READI*ness will enable you to lead yourself so that you can effectively lead your team and manage the business entrusted to you.

I wish you success on your professional journey. I hope that what I have shared provided insight to support your leadership into the future, that the tools discussed are a good start to your leadership toolbox. I hope the resources I mentioned give you enough of a tease that you search further to explore and learn more about the wisdom of so many great leaders. I wish you joy in your pursuit of excellence. I leave you with one more thought from another guru, a quote from Confucius, "The will to win, the desire to succeed, the urge to reach your full potential...these are the keys that will unlock the door to personal excellence." **Shine your light and inspire others to shine their light**. Lead *READI* to make a difference for the people you lead and the patients in your care.

Works Cited

American Organization of Nursing Leadership:
https://www.aonl.org/about/overview

ANCC, (n.d.). *Magnet Model: Creating a Magnet Culture.* Retrieved from:
https://www.nursingworld.org/organizational-
programs/magnet/magnet-model/

ANA, (2015). *Guide to the Code of Ethics for Nurses with Interpretive Statements:
Development, Interpretation, and Application, 2nd Edition.* Silver Spring MD.
ANA.

ANA. (2014). *Nursing: Scope and Standards of Practice, 3rd Ed.* Silver Spring
MD. ANA

Anderson, R.A., & McDaniel, R.R. (2000). Managing health care
organizations: where professionalism meets complexity science. *Health
Care Management Review,* 25(1): 83-92.

AONE, AONL. (2015). *AONL Nurse Manager Competencies.* Chicago, IL:
AONE, AONL.

Arndt, M. & Bigelow, B. (2000). Commentary: The potential of chaos
theory and complexity theory for health services management. *Health Care
Management Review,* 25(1); 35-38.

Benner, P.J. (2001). *From novice to expert, excellence and power in clinical nursing
practice.* Prentice-Hall, Inc: Upper Saddle River, NJ.

Bianco, C., Dudkiewicz, P.B., Lenerre, D. (2014). Building nurse leader
relationships. *Nursing Management,* Volume :45 Number 5 , page 42 - 48

Blanchard, K. H. & Broadwell, R. (2018). *Servant Leadership in action: How
you can achieve great relationships and results.* Berrett-Koehler Publishing Inc.:
San Francisco, CA.

Blanchard, K.H. & Hodges, P. (2003). *Servant Leadership transforming your heart, head, hands and habits.* Thomas Nelson. United States.

Blanchard, K.H. & Miller, M. (2004), *The Secret: what great leaders know and do.* Berrett-Koehler Publishing Inc.: San Francisco, CA.

Brown, B. (2015). *Rising strong, how the ability to reset transforms the way we live, love, parent and lead.* Penguin Random House, LLC: New York, NY.

Brown, B. (2018). *Dare to lead, Brave work. Tough conversations. Whole hearts.* Penguin Random House, LLC: New York, NY.

Bruch, H. & Ghoshal, S. (2002). Beware the busy manager. *Harvard Business Review.* Retrieved from: https://hbr.org/2002/02/beware-the-busy-manager

Chaffee, M.W. & McNeill, M.M. RN, (2007). A model of nursing as a complex adaptive system. *Nursing Outlook:* vol 55, is 5, 232-241.

Chapman, E. (2009). *Radical loving care: Building the healing hospital in America.* Baptist Healing Trust: Nashville, TN.

Chapman, (2009). *Sacred work: Planting cultures of radical loving care in America.* Baptist Healing Trust: Nashville, TN.

Clavelle, J. T., O'Grady, T. P. & Drenkard, K. (2013). Structural empowerment and the nursing practice environment in Magnet organizations. *The Journal of Nursing Administration:* Volume 43 - Issue 11 - p 566-573

Cialdini, R.B. (2001). Harnessing the science of persuasion. *Harvard Business Review.* Retrieved from: https://hbr.org/2001/10/harnessing-the-science-of-persuasion

Clifton, D. & Nelson, P. (1992). *Soar with your strengths.* Delacorte Press: New York, NY.

Coffman, C.W. & Sorenson, K. (2013). *Culture eats strategy for lunch: The secret of extraordinary results, igniting the passion within.* Denver, CO: Liang Addison Press.

Collins, J. (2001). *Good to Great: Why Some Companies Make the Leap and Others Don't.* HarperCollins Publishing: New York, NY

Conner, D. R. (2006). *Managing at the Speed of Change.* Random House Inc.: New York, NY.

Connerpartners (2011). *The Eight Stages of Building Commitment.* Retrieved from: https://www.connerpartners.com/blog-posts-containing-downloadable-tools/the-eight-stages-of-building-commitment

Conscious Leadership Group: https://conscious.is/

Corkindale, G. (2007). How to manage conflict. *Harvard Business Review.* Retrieved from: https://hbr.org/2007/11/how-to-manage-conflict

Covey, S. R. (1989). *The 7 habits of highly effective people.* Free Press: Glencoe, IL.

Delong, T.J. (2011). *Flying Without a Net: Turn Fear of Change into Fuel for Success.* Harvard Business School Publishing: Boston, MA.

Delong, T.J. (2011). *Three Questions for Effective Feedback. Harvard Business Review.* Retrieved from: https://hbr.org/2011/08/three-questions-for-effective-feedback

Derby, E. & Larsen, D. (2006). *Agile Retrospectives: Making Good Teams Great.* Pragmatic Bookshelf: United States.

Dethmer, J. (2015). *5 Keys to being conscious in conflict.* Conscious Leadership Group. Retrieved from: https://conscious.is/blogs/5-keys-to-being-conscious-in-conflict#:~:text=Destructive%20conflict%20occurs%20when%20stakeholders,right%20that%20causes%20dysfunctional%20conflict.

Dethmer, J., Chapman, D. & Warner Klemp, K. (2014). *The 15 commitments of conscious leadership: A new paradigm for sustainable success.* Dethmer, Chapman & Klemp: ISBN-13 9780990976905

DeWolf, D. (2011). *It's not about getting the right people on the bus.* Retrieved from: https://daviddewolf.com/its-not-about-getting-the-right-people-on-the-bus/

Dohman, E.L. (2009). *Accountability in nursing: Six strategies to build and maintain a culture of commitment.* HCPro, Inc: Danvers, MA.

Drucker, P.F. (2002). They're not employees, they're people. *Harvard Business Review.* Retrieved from: https://hbr.org/2002/02/theyre-not-employees-theyre-people

Eurich, T. (2018). What self-awareness really is (and how to cultivate it). *Harvard Business Review.* Retrieved from: https://hbr.org/2018/01/what-self-awareness-really-is-and-how-to-cultivate-it

Gabarro, J. J. & Kotter, J. P. (2005). Managing your boss. *Harvard Business Review.* Retrieved from: https://hbr.org/2005/01/managing-your-boss

Galbraith, J. R. (1995). *Designing organizations: an executive briefing on strategy, structure and process.* San Francisco: Jossey-Bass.

Galloway, D. (2016). Control or Caring? What is your motive for a safety conversation? Continuous Mile. Retrieved from: https://www.continuousmile.com/behavior/control-or-caring-safety-conversation/

Gawande, A. (2009). *Checklist manifesto: How to get things right.* Metropolitan Books: New York, NY.

Garfinkle, J. (n.d.a.). *Building positive relationships at work.* Retrieved from: https://garfinkleexecutivecoaching.com/articles/build-positive-work-relationships/building-positive-relationships-at-work accessed January 8, 2021.

Glaveski, S. (2019). Where companies go wrong with learning and development. *Harvard Business Review*. Retrieved from: https://hbr.org/2019/10/where-companies-go-wrong-with-learning-and-development

Goffee, R. & Jones, G. (2005). Managing authenticity: The paradox of great leadership. *Harvard Business Review*. Retrieved from: https://hbr.org/2005/12/managing-authenticity-the-paradox-of-great-leadership

Goldsmith, M. & Reiter, M. (2007). *What got you here won't get you there: how successful people become even more successful*. Hyperion: New York, NY.

Goleman, D. (2004). What makes a leader. *Harvard Business Review*. Retrieved from: https://hbr.org/2004/01/what-makes-a-leader

Greenleaf, R.K. (2015) *The servant as leader* [pamphlet revised edition]. The Greenleaf Center for Servant Leadership.

Greenleaf, R.K. Center for servant leadership. https://www.greenleaf.org/robert-k-greenleaf-biography/

Greenleaf, R.K. & Spears, L.(1998). *The power of servant leadership*. Berrett-Koehler Publishers, Inc: San Francisco, CA.

Grenny, J., Patterson, K., Maxfield, D., McMillan, R. & Switzler, A. (2013). Influencer: The new science of leading change. McGraw-Hill: New York, NY.

Grote, D. (2011). *How to be good at performance appraisals: simple, effective, done right*. Harvard Business School Publishing: Boston, MA.

Hallenbeck, G.S. & Eichenger, R. W. (2006). *Interviewing right: How science can sharpen your interviewing accuracy*. Lominger International: Minneapolis, MN.

The Health Foundation, (2010). *Complex adaptive systems.* Retrieved from: https://www.health.org.uk/sites/default/files/ComplexAdaptiveSystems.pdf

Hiatt, J. (nda). *What is the ADKAR Model.* Retrieved from: https://www.prosci.com/adkar/adkar-model

Hiatt, J. M. (2006). *ADKAR: a model for change in business, government and our community.* Prosci Learning Center Publications: Loveland, CO.

Hill, L.A. (2007). Becoming the boss. *Harvard Business Review.* Retrieved from: https://hbr.org/2007/01/becoming-the-boss

Holland, J.H. (20007). Studying complex adaptive systems. *Journal of Systems Science and Complexity.* 19, 1–8. Retrieved from: https://doi.org/10.1007/s11424-006-0001-z

Howard, T. (2007). *Untie the knots that tie up your life, a practical guide to freeing yourself from toxic choices people relationships.* Knotts Free Publishing: Baltimore, MD.

Ibarra, H. (2015). The authenticity paradox: Why feeling like a fake can be a sign of growth. *Harvard Business Review.* Retrieved from: https://hbr.org/2015/01/the-authenticity-paradox

Ibarra, H. & Hunter, M.L. (20017). How leaders create and use networks. *Harvard Business Review.* Retrieved from: https://hbr.org/2007/01/how-leaders-create-and-use-networks

IHI. (). *How to Improve.* Retrieved from: http://www.ihi.org/resources/Pages/HowtoImprove/default.aspx

Institute of Medicine. (2011). *The future of nursing: Leading change ,advancing health.* The National Academies Press: Washington DC.

Kaye, B. & Jordan-Evans, S. (2005). *Love'em or lose'em: Getting good people to stay.* Barrett-Koehler Publishing: San Francisco, CA.

Koloroutis, M. (2004). *Relationship-based care: A model for transforming practice.* Creative Health Care Management. Minneapolis, MN.

Koloroutis, M. & Abelson, D. (2017). *Advancing relationship-based cultures.* States: Creative Health Care Management. Minneapolis, MN.

Kotter, J.P. (2012). *Leading Change.* Harvard Business Press: Boston, MA

Kotter, J.P. (2014). *Accelerate: Building Strategic Agility for a Faster-Moving World.* Harvard Business Press: Boston, MA

Kotter, J.P. & Cohen, D. S. (2002). *Heart of Change: Real-Life Stories of How People Change Their Organizations.* Harvard Business Press: Boston, MA

Kotter, J.P. & Rathgeber, H. (2005). *Our iceberg is melting: Changing and succeeding under any conditions.* St Martin's Press: New York, NY.

Kouzes, J.M. & Posner, B.Z. (2011). *Credibility, how leaders gain and lose it; Why people demand it.* Jossey-Bass: San Francisco, CA.

Kouzes, J.M. & Posner, B.Z. (2003). *Encouraging the heart: A leaders guide to rewarding and recognizing others.* Jossey-Bass: San Francisco, CA.

Kouzes, J.M. & Posner, B.Z. (2017). *The leadership challenge: How to make extraordinary things happen in organizations.* John Wiley & Sons, Inc.: Hoboken, NJ

Kramer M., Schmalenberg C., Maguire P. (2010). Nine structures and leadership practices essential for a magnetic (healthy) work environment. *Nursing Administration Quarterly.* 34(1):4-17.

Larrabee, J. H., Withrow, M. L., Janney, M. A., Hobbs, G. R., Ostrow, C. L., & Burant, C. (2003). Predicting registered nurse job satisfaction and intent to leave. *Journal of Nursing Administration,* 33(5), 271-283.

Laschinger, H. K. S., Finegan, J., Shamian, J., & Wilk, P. (2001). Impact of structural and psychological empowerment on job strain in nursing work settings: Expanding Kanter's model. *Journal of Nursing Administration,* 31, 260-272.

Laschinger, H. K. S., Finegan, J., Shamian, J., & Wilk, P. (2004). A longitudinal analysis of the impact of workplace empowerment on work satisfaction. *Journal of Organizational Behavior*, 25(4), 527.

Laschinger, H. K. S., Shamian, J., & Thomson, D. (2001). Impact of magnet hospital characteristics on nurses' perceptions of hospital burnout, quality of care and work satisfaction. *Nursing Economics*, 19, 209-219.

Lean Enterprise Institute. https://www.lean.org/

Leggat, S. G., Bartram, T., Casimir, G. & Stanton, P. (2010). Nurse perceptions of the quality of patient care: Confirming the importance of empowerment and job satisfaction. *Health Care Management Review*. Volume 35 - Issue 4 - p 355-364

Leis J.A, & Shojania, K. G. (2017). A primer on PDSA: executing plan–do–study–act cycles in practice, not just in name. *BMJ Quality & Safety*, 26:572-577.

Lencioni, P. (2002). *The five dysfunctions of a team*. Jossey-Bass: San Francisco, CA

Lencioni, P. (2012). *The advantage: why organizational health trumps everything else in business*. Jossey-Bass: San Francisco, CA

Lipman. V. (2017). *66% of employees would quit if they feel unappreciated*. Forbes. Retrieved from: https://www.forbes.com/sites/victorlipman/2017/04/15/66-of-employees-would-quit-if-they-feel-unappreciated/?sh=316a21996897

Manojlovich, M. & Spence Laschinger, H. (2002). The relationship of empowerment and selected personality characteristics to nursing job satisfaction. *Journal of Nursing Administration*: Volume 32 - Issue 11 - p 586-595

Marquet, L. D. (2012). Turn the ship around: A true story of tuning followers into leaders. Penguin Group: New York, NY.

Maxwell, J. (2007). *The 21 irrefutable laws of leadership.* Thomas Nelson, Inc: Nashville, TN.

Mele, C., Pels, J. Polese, F. (2010). A brief review of systems theories and their managerial applications. *Service Science* 2(1-2):126-135. Retrieved from: https://pubsonline.informs.org/doi/pdf/10.1287/serv.2.1_2.126

Morgan, A. Lynch, C. & Lynch, S. (2017) *Spark: How to lead yourself and others to greater success.* Houghton Mifflin Harcourt Publishing: New York, NY.

Morrison, R. S., Jones, L., & Fuller, B. (1997). The relation between leadership style and empowerment on job satisfaction of nurses. *Journal of Nursing Administration,* 27(5), 27-34.a

Mosswarner *(n.d.a.).How to engage your employees in embracing change…Meet people where they are.* Retrieved from: https://newsfeed.mosswarner.com/change-management-communications/ accessed January 16, 2021.

Nummenmaaa,L., Glereana, E., Harib,R. &, Hietanen, J.K. (2014). Bodily maps of emotions. *Proceedings of the National Academy of Sciences.* Jan 2014, 111 (2) 646-651; DOI: 10.1073/pnas.1321664111

Neal, J.E. (2009). *Effective phrases for performance appraisals: A guide to successful evaluations, 12th Edition.* Neal Publishing: Perrysburg, OH

Nelson, B. (2012). 1501 *Ways to reward employees.* Workman Publishing Company: New York, NY

Ngo, K. (2013). *Let's Do This! 100 Motivational Messages to Inspire Action.* Create Space Independent Publishing Platform: United States.

Ning, S., Zhong, H., Libo, W., & Qiujie, L. (2009). The impact of nurse empowerment on job satisfaction. *Journal of Advanced Nursing,* 65(12), 2642-2648.

NSI Nursing Solutions (2020). *2021 NSI national health care retention & RN staffing report*. NSI Nursing Solutions, Inc. Retrieved from: https://www.nsinursingsolutions.com/Documents/Library/NSI_Nation al_Health_Care_Retention_Report.pdf

Oettingen, G. (2014). *Rethinking positive thinking*. Penguin Random House: New York, NY.

Oncken, W. Wass, D.L. & Covey, S.R. (1999). Management time: Who's got the monkey. *Harvard Business Review*. Retrieved from: https://hbr.org/1999/11/management-time-whos-got-the-monkey

Onuoha, I. E. (2011). *Overcoming the challenges of life*. Author House: Bloomington, IN.

Patterson, K., Grenny, J. McMillan, R. & Switzler, A. (2002). *Crucial conversations: Tools for talking when the stakes are high*. McGraw Hill: New York, NY.

Patterson, K., Grenny, J. McMillan, R. & Switzler, A. (2002). *Crucial confrontations: Tools for resolving broken promises, violated expectations and bad behavior*. McGraw Hill: New York, NY.

Peek, S. (2020). 6 Tips for Writing an Effective Performance Review. *Business News Daily*. Retrieved from: https://www.businessnewsdaily.com/5760-write-good-performance-review.html

Penprase, B. & Norris, D. (2005). What Nurse Leaders Should Know About Complex Adaptive Systems Theory. *Nursing Leadership Forum:* 9(3) 127-32.

Posner, B. (2015). *Why credibility is the foundation of leadership*. TEDx. University of Nevada. Retrieved from: https://www.youtube.com/watch?v=QmMcSBQvQLQ

Prichard, S. (2018). *The book of mistakes: 9 secrets to creating a successful future.* Hachett Book Group: New York, NY.

Press Ganey and Associates, Inc (2017). *2017 Press Ganey Nursing Special Report, The Influence of Nurse Manager Leadership on Patient and Nurse Outcomes and the Mediating Effects of the Nurse Work Environment.* South Bend, IN

ProjectManager. (n.d.a.). Retrieved from: https://www.projectmanager.com/ accessed January 16, 2021.

Pype, P., Mertens, F., Helewaut, F. & Krystallidou, D. (2018). Healthcare teams as complex adaptive systems: understanding team behaviour through team members' perception of interpersonal interaction. *BMC Health Services Research.* Retrieved from: https://bmchealthservres.biomedcentral.com/articles/10.1186/s12913-018-3392-3?optIn=false

Ramos-Villagrasa, P.J., Marques-Quinteiro, P., Navarro, J. & Rico, R. (2017). *Teams as complex adaptive systems: Reviewing 17 years of research.* Retrieved from: https://doi.org/10.1177/1046496417713849

Rath, T. (2007). *StrengthsFinder 2.0.* Gallop Press: New York, NY.

Reid, E. & Ramarajan, l. (2016). Managing the high intensity workplace: An "always available" culture breeds a variety of dysfunctional behaviors. *Harvard Business Review.* Retrieved from: https://hbr.org/2016/06/managing-the-high-intensity-workplace

Rogers, R. M. (2016). Even the long ranger didn't do it alone. *West Michigan Christian News.* Retrieved from: https://www.westmichiganchristian.com/local/528-even-the-lone-ranger-didn-t-go-it-alone.html

Robbins, T. (1991). *Awaken the giant within : How to take immediate control of your mental, emotional, physical and financial destiny.* Simon & Schuster: New York, NY.

Ropella, P. B. (2013). These key components lead to effective communication. *Happi.* Retrieved from: https://www.happi.com/issues/2013-02/view_human-capital-management/these-key-components-lead-to-effective-communication/

Schaubhut, N. A. (2007). Technical brief fort he Thomas-Killmann conflict mode instrument: Description of the updated normative sample and implications for use. *CPP, Inc.* Retrieved from: http://www.honeconsulting.com/wp-content/uploads/2015/10/TKI-Technical-Brief.pdf

Schien, E.H. (2013). *Humble inquiry: The gentle art of asking instead of telling.* Berrett-Koehler Publishers: Oakland CA.

Schwartz, T. & McCarthy, C. (2007). Manage your energy not your time. *Harvard Business Review.* Retrieved from: https://hbr.org/2007/10/manage-your-energy-not-your-time

Sinek, S. (2009). *Start with why: How great leaders inspire everyone to take action.* Penguin Random House: New York, NY.

Sinek, S. (2017). *Leaders eat last: why some teams pull together and others don't.* Penguin Random House: New York, NY.

Sinek, S. (2020). *Who comes first: You or the group?* Retrieved from: https://www.youtube.com/watch?v=p349WK88SQo

Stadler, G. & Oettingen, G. (2010). Intervention effects of information and self-regulation on eating fruits and vegetables over two years. *Health Psychology,* 29(3), 274-283.

Stadler, G. Oettingen, G. & Gollwitzer, P.M. (2009). Physical activity in women: Effects of a self-regulation intervention. *American Journal of Preventive Medicine,* 36(1), 29-34.

Stainer, M.B. (2016). *The coaching habit: say less, ask more & change the way you lead forever.* Box of Crayons: Toronto, Canada.

Studer Group. (2010). *The nurse leader handbook: the art and science of nurse leadership.* Fire Starter Publishing: Gulf Breeze, FL.

Sullivan, J. (2016). 7 rules for job interview questions that result in great hires. *Harvard Business Review.* Retrieved from: https://hbr.org/2016/02/7-rules-for-job-interview-questions-that-result-in-great-hires

Sullivan, T. (2011). Embracing complexity. *Harvard Business Review.* Retrieved from: https://hbr.org/2011/09/embracing-complexity

Theodorou, M. (2020). 9 reasons why employees quit their jobs. *Career Addict.* Retrieved from: https://www.careeraddict.com/why-employees-quit

Thomas, K. W. (2002). *Introduction to conflict management: Improving performance using the TKI.* CPP, Inc.: Mountain View, CA:

Toussaint, J. & Gerard, R.A. (2010). *On the mend, revolutionizing healthcare to save lives and transform the industry.* Lean Enterprise Institute: Cambridge, MA.

Verble, D. (2015). *Practical guidance for using humble inquiry in PDCA problem solving and coaching.* Lean Enterprise Institute. Retrieved from: https://www.lean.org/common/display/?o=3109

Wagner, J.I.J., Cummings, G., Smith, D. L., Olson, J., Anderson, L. & Warren, S. (2010). The relationship between structural empowerment and psychological empowerment for nurses: a systematic review. *Journal of Nursing Management* 18, 448–462

Walker, C.A. (2002). Saving your rookie manager from themselves. *Harvard Business Review*. Retrieved from: https://hbr.org/2002/04/saving-your-rookie-managers-from-themselves

Watkins, M.D. (2013). *The First 90 Days Proven Strategies for Getting Up to Speed Faster and Smarter.* Boston, MA. *Harvard Business Review* Press.

Watkins, M.D. (2012). How managers become leaders. *Harvard Business Review*. Retrieved from: https://hbr.org/2012/06/how-managers-become-leaders

Watkins, M.D. (2015). Leading the team you inherit: It's not the same a building one from scratch. *Harvard Business Review*. Retrieved from: https://hbr.org/2016/06/leading-the-team-you-inherit

Wignall, N. (2019). The Elements of Self-Reflection. *The Understanding Project*. Retrieved from:

https://medium.com/the-understanding-project/the-elements-of-self-reflection-cdf7aa70ed2e

Womack, J.P. & Jones, D.T. (1996). *Lean thinking: Banish waste and create wealth in your corporation.* Simon & Schuster: New York, NY.

Wong C.A. & Cummings G.G. (2007) The relationship between nursing leadership and patient outcomes: a systematic review. *Journal of Nursing Management* 15 (5), 508–521.

Wong C.A. & Cummings G.G. (2009) The influence of authentic leadership behaviours on trust and work outcomes in healthcare staff. *Journal of Leadership Studies* 3 (2), 6–23.

Wong C.A., Cummings G.G. & Ducharme L. (2013) The relationship between nursing leadership and patient outcomes: a systematic review update. *Journal of Nursing Management 21, 709–724.*

About the Author

Lisa Gossett has over 30 years of leadership experience in nursing and hospital operations. She has held various leadership roles of increasing responsibility, including a senior executive role at a healthcare system where she had strategic oversight of more than 10,000 nursing associates across 12 hospitals, 200+ ambulatory locations, home health and hospice.

Lisa is founder of Gossett Consulting & Insights, LLC where she provides assessment, feedback and coaching to fine-tune skills of leaders of all levels. Her business is a culmination of decades of mentoring others and encouraging individuals and teams to examine desires, challenge choices and uncover their full potential. She is known for maximizing the capability of those around her. She develops individuals and teams to accomplish what they had not previously conceived. Lisa coaches clients in transition to support success in a new role as well as established leaders to achieve goals creating success for themselves, their teams, and their organizations. The mission of Gossett Consulting & Insights is to support leaders at all levels as they fully discover their own light so they can inspire the light in others.

As showcased through Lisa's development of the R.E.A.D.I. to Lead model, she is committed to supporting and investing in the development of frontline managers leading at the point of care. It is through the inspiration of leaders at the point of care that patients feel cared for and cared about during precious moments in their lives. She believes that supporting these individuals is vital to shift paradigms and improve care delivery.

Lisa lives in central Ohio with her husband, two dogs, five cats and paddling of ducks. She has two children and is "Mimzi" to four (soon to be five) grandchildren. Lisa's faith, family and small-town roots keep her grounded, and her constant curiosity helps her discover new insights. Her foundation as a nurse and the mentors who invested in her career helped cultivate her personal purpose to help others become the best version of themselves. She believes in the value of every person and loves the opportunity to discover the extraordinariness of anyone she meets.

linkedin.com/in/lisa-gossett
www.gossettinsights.com
Lisa@gossettinsights.com

Made in the USA
Monee, IL
10 March 2022

92676101R00173